OWN
A RACEHORSE
Without Spending a Fortune

OWN
A RACEHORSE
Without Spending a Fortune

Partnering in the Sport of Kings

HAROLD METZEL

ECLIPSE PRESS

Lexington, Kentucky

Library of Congress Control Number: 2003102042

ISBN 1-58150-100-5

Printed in the United States
First Edition: October 2003

Distributed to the trade by
National Book Network
4501 Forbes Boulevard, Suite 200, Lanham, MD 20706
1.800.462.6420

a division of
Blood-Horse Publications
PUBLISHERS SINCE 1916

ECLIPSE
PRESS

Contents

Preface

T hree years ago a friend invited me to visit the backside of the track at Del Mar, California, to see his racehorses up close. Standing next to those gorgeous Thoroughbreds, which represent the best of their species at their athletic prime, I was awed. The sights, smells, and activity I encountered ushered me into a world I'd never before seen.

Here, I met the trainers, jockeys, and owners who make this sport happen. I'd accepted my friend's invitation out of curiosity but within a few hours was also intoxicated. I had always believed you had to be rich to own a racehorse. Now I learned it was possible to own a percentage interest in one or more horses for just a few thousand dollars. On the spot I decided to give it a try.

That first investment yielded mixed results. One of my three horses won her first and second races, and we later sold her for twice her purchase price. The other two never made it to the starting gate. Overall, my venture was close to a breakeven proposition.

The real disappointment in that first try, however, was discovering that although my trainer (whose real name I will not use in the book) may have been skilled at training horses, he was a poor businessman and our relationship ended. Nevertheless, the sweet taste of success and the thrill of watching my own horse drive toward the finish line to outpace her competition had me hooked. So I needed to find a new trainer/partner.

My search for a published guidebook proved fruitless. Taking matters into my own hands, I personally queried the 262 entities that offered partnerships in the resource directory known as *The Source*, published by *The Blood-Horse* magazine. From this effort I learned about the many types of partnerships, how much investment was required, and which proposals were well-thought-out offerings. Since then, I've selected two managing partners and have had very satisfying results.

In the past few years, I have become more involved by educating myself about the entire scope of the industry. I visited several racetracks, breeding farms, and auctions as well as interviewed trainers and owners. I also attended almost a dozen seminars put on by organizations that encourage ownership, such as the Thoroughbred Owners and Breeders Association and the Thoroughbred Owners of California. Although these seminars were helpful, and there are a good number of very helpful resources available, I could not find a published volume to answer my questions and guide me into the further involvement I sought. That is what motivated me to write this book.

It is my hope that within a few hours, you'll understand the basics and be encouraged that you, too, can own a Thoroughbred racehorse without spending a fortune. And you can bet on this: there is no thrill like walking up to your own horse just before race time, patting her on the neck, and whispering some encouraging words in her ear. Then when she breaks from the gate...Oh my! You can't believe the emotion that floods your heart.

It's worth it, friend. So let's take a look at what's involved in ownership for you. I hope you decide to give it a try. And one day, maybe we'll stand together at the rail shouting, "Go, baby, go!"

Harold Metzel
June 2003

1

A Reason to Believe

In the past few years I've become part owner of several Thoroughbred racehorses by buying a percentage interest in them. This type of involvement has taught me that you don't have to be wealthy to enjoy the excitement of ownership. And now I'd like to encourage you to give it a try. Is the risk reasonable? I think so. Without spending a fortune, you can have fun and, with sound judgment, make a profit.

In the next few pages, you'll see how I came to discover a reason to believe.

The Birth of a Horseman

"Steady, girl." My hand caressed Pert Laura's long, sleek neck in an effort to calm her. This was the filly's first race, and she was wired. Her nostrils flared and her eyes darted around the paddock area, taking in all the activity.

Her trainer, Richie Farrell, stood next to us, relaxed and natural, as he gave last-minute instructions to the jockey, J.G. Matos.

"You know her pretty well, J.G. She's a bit nervous right now, but once you get her onto the track she'll know it's a race. Her morning workouts have shown us that she likes to win. Let her set her own pace as long as you think she isn't trying to do too much too early. And go easy on the whip unless you see something developing."

"Yes, sir. Our little lass is in good shape, and we're only going six."

Six furlongs is three-fourths of a mile, a good distance for a two-year-old just starting her racing career, especially as it was only August, pretty early in the racing year for such a young horse.

It seemed impossible that less than five weeks ago, I had accompanied my friend Richard to the backside of the track in Del Mar, California, and looked up close at a Thoroughbred for the very first time. I accepted my friend's invitation to join him and watch the horses work out early in the morning because of his enthusiasm and interest in the horses he owned a percentage interest in. I knew almost nothing of the sport.

Pert Laura had been one of three horses grouped in a single partnership. Although I had never before heard of owning horses in partnership, before the day was out I had purchased a 10 percent interest in a group of three two-year-olds in training. Pert Laura was the first of the three to develop into race-ready condition.

Farrell trained a number of horses, and with all of his assigned stalls full, he housed this young filly in an outside stall that resembled a large, metal cage. When we walked over so I could get my first look at this prospect that morning, she raised her head and stared back at us, her ears alert and swiveling.

Her coat, almost black, glistened. She stood tall and regal, assessing the situation and wondering what we were about. Her big, beautiful eyes shined with intelligence. I was captivated. Please understand that my experience with horses had been limited to an occasional rented hour on a tired and bored horse. Standing before me now was a different type of animal.

As Farrell explained to me what ownership would entail, Pert Laura stuck her head over the top railing to allow us to stroke her nose and head. I reached through the bars to pet her and felt the satin softness of her nose. I never would have believed when I got out of bed that morning that by noon I would own a piece of not only Pert Laura but also two other Thoroughbred racehorses.

After that first day on the backside, I returned a couple of times to watch my horses train and then attend the races. When the track season at Del Mar concluded, I thought the excitement was over for a while. Then just two weeks later, and with just two days' notice, Farrell called to tell me that he had entered Pert Laura in a race. She would be running at Fairplex Park in Pomona, which is in the Los Angeles area. He called all of the owners so we could attend, if possible. If possible? I lived in San Diego at the time and would have hiked the one hundred plus miles to L.A. for this experience.

On race day, I was in the paddock, stroking Pert Laura again and telling her that we knew she could do it, and that she should just relax, and other such nonsense. This is, after all, just a horse that can't understand English,

I told myself. But at a time like that you don't want to think rationally. I was pumped!

"I'm putting a bundle down on this beauty," said Dave, one of my new partners, who like myself was a rookie. "She looks great, and I think she's ready."

Though eight of us owned a percentage interest in this young filly, only a few of us were allowed in the paddock at a time. The group decided that Dave and I, as the neophytes, should experience hearing the trainer's last-minute instructions to the jockey and offer our best wishes to our would-be champion.

On other days when I had gone to the races, I stood outside the paddock and watched the horses get saddled and then parade around the ring. Only owners, trainers, and jockeys are allowed inside this grassy enclosure. As an owner, here I was standing on the perfectly manicured grass as the large crowd stood outside the paddock pressed in to examine the horses about to go head to head.

The paddock judge called for "riders up." Farrell took hold of J.G.'s left foot and gave him a leg up. We watched the horses walk around the ring once more, and then they headed out to the track.

Almost immediately we heard the trumpeter announce the call to post with the familiar tune of "First Call." That cavalry call has to be one of the most recognized refrains associated with sports. We joined the other trainers and owners as they followed the procession of horses out through the gap in the grandstand onto the track. Ten minutes remained until post time.

As we came out of the gap, the sunlight blinded us a bit, but we saw our partners waiting for us, all smiles and thumbs up. We had agreed to gather on the observation platform for this race, either to celebrate or commiserate together. As we joined our group, everyone started asking questions at once. "What was it like?" "What did Richie say to the jockey?" "How did she look, Dave? Think she can do it today?"

Some of our partners had been involved in racing for a long time. Others, like Dave and me, were still learning our way around. Each of us had invested a different amount in our three-horse partnership, but we all shared the same vision. I'd only known these people for a short time and yet felt like I was part of a special club or a family.

The butterflies occupying my stomach the past few days had multiplied as we awaited our race, the eighth one of the day. Although ignorant about the strategies involved, I learned not only that this was our filly's first race, but that our jockey was also an apprentice. I would have been more comfortable hearing that a seasoned pro was taking her on her first trip, but I rested in the knowledge that Farrell, our trainer and managing partner, knew what he was doing.

As the tote board began lighting up for our race, I was encouraged to see that Pert Laura and a horse named Sheer were the favorites. Just before post time, the bettors wavered and Pert Laura's odds increased to 3-1, while Sheer and another horse were the favorites with odds of 5-2.

The distinctive voice of track announcer Trevor Denman came over the speakers, "The horses are approaching the starting gate." Time slowed down as we waited for the nine horses to be loaded, one by one, into their respective starting positions. Finally we heard, "They're in."

We didn't, however, want to hear what he said next.

"Pert Laura is restless."

With the starting gate across the oval from the grandstand, we couldn't see the horses being loaded. We all held our breath, knowing how easily a horse can be injured in the starting gate.

The track announcer carried more unsettling news. "Pert Laura, rearing up in the gate...has unseated the rider." Denman paused, "Settling, Pert Laura. Now, Charismatic Two is getting restless." He paused again while we waited. Finally we heard, "The rider of Pert Laura is okay, climbing back up." Our lungs resumed their normal function.

Several of the horses fought their jockeys and resisted entering the gate. All of them were young with few to no races under their girths. It took another fifteen seconds or so until we heard the bell ring, the gates crash open, and Trevor's famous phrase, "Annnd, away they go."

Within seconds we saw Pert Laura, third from last. She soon overtook one horse but pretty much stayed in the fifth position, about seven lengths off the lead, for the majority of the race.

Halfway around the final turn, the jockey told her to step on it, and she responded beautifully. With just a few strides, she overtook two more horses and now sat third off the leader. As the horses came around the turn, Pert Laura was forced to give up a step to get around the second horse and into the outside lane. Once there, seeing no more obstacles, the jockey asked her for speed by lightly tapping her twice with the whip.

It was exciting. I actually saw her pin her ears, lower her head, and lengthen her stride as she kicked into gear. Sheer had led since the starting gate opened, and now Pert Laura had a bead on her. Sheer saw her coming and picked up the pace but not fast enough. Pert Laura flew past the horse in second and pressed on past Sheer to beat her by a neck at the wire.

Talk about celebration! Talk about excited! We danced and whooped and

BILL SCHERUS

PERT LAURA   FAIRPLEX PARK - POMONA, CA
                    September 18, 1997   Purse: $17,000
Owner: TEAM FLEET STABLE, JACOBS SALM, ET AL

Pert Laura's partners celebrate in the winner's circle.

hugged each other. One of the women started crying. Larry, the big guy in our group, gave me a high-five and said, "Damn, that was fun!"

We had gathered on the observation platform in front of the grandstand because it is near the winner's circle. As the horses cooled down and returned to the front side of the track, we had plenty of time to get down and assemble for a picture with our winner. Giddy as school children, we skipped down the steps with fans from all over the place slapping us on the back or shouting their congratulations.

My memory of our time in the winner's circle remains a blur. Farrell came around and shook hands with each of us; the photographer waited for the jockey to bring Pert Laura up in front of the group and snapped the shot. Then it was over.

I found my way back to my seat and basked in a fantastical aura. Five weeks ago I had never been to the backside of a track, had only attended a race meet a couple of times, and had never even considered owning a race-horse. Here I was now not only an owner but also the owner of a winner. My filly was on her way back to the barn having won 60 percent of a $17,000 purse, and this was just at the start of her career. I didn't know what to think about all that. It was one of the most exciting times I've ever had, and it demonstrated the reason people get so caught up in racing these beautiful horses. There is simply nothing like it.

I was hooked!

2

What Are Thoroughbred Partnerships?

When a person is first approached about buying an interest in a Thoroughbred, the most common reaction is, "Me? Own a racehorse? I don't think so!" Maybe you, too, thought it not possible. Well, here's the good news. Other people, just like you, would also like to get involved but want to limit the cash they have to lay on the line.

In a partnership, several people pool their money in exchange for a corresponding percentage of a horse or horses. The partners share proportionately in costs, winnings, and whatever profit or fame may come from the endeavor. As racehorses are quite expensive, owning a percentage interest makes involvement much more affordable and attainable.

Advantages of Buying a Racehorse in Partnership

Joining a partnership makes enormous sense for someone just getting started in the business. The advantages of partnerships over sole ownership include the following: sharing costs; the opportunity to diversify; a professional to oversee the management of your horse while you are learning the ABCs of a new business; and the special satisfaction of discussing issues and celebrating victories with your partners.

Sharing Costs

The most expensive part of racehorse ownership is not the acquisition but the upkeep. You can buy a racehorse, believe it or not, for as little as a thousand dollars. (Of course, most cost several thousand dollars or a lot more if you're shopping for a world-class pedigree.) However, all horses, no matter how much they cost, require adequate food and housing, medical attention, and ongoing training. This costly maintenance often exceeds the purchase price and must be carefully considered when you are buying a horse or an interest in one.

The average cost of maintaining a horse at a racetrack, including the trainer's fee, food, stabling, etc., will range between $55 and $75 a day. On average then let's say it will cost approximately $2,000 per month to maintain a horse at a racetrack or about $24,000 per year.

Even when sharing the bills with partners, it is important to keep in mind your percentage of the costs. And don't count on any revenue the first year. If your horse begins winning races straight out of the gate, that's wonderful. Just don't count on it. So, if the partnership buys a horse for $20,000, add in the estimated $24,000 for expenses. If you are buying a 10 percent interest, you'll only have to come up with $2,000 at the time of purchase. But you'll need to set aside the additional $2,400 for ongoing maintenance costs. If you don't, you could find yourself in an uncomfortable situation.

Costs will also vary depending upon where your horse is boarded: tracks cost more than farms, big cities more than smaller communities, and coasts more than mid-country.

During its lifetime a horse will be kept at a horse farm, the racetrack, or a training facility (often a horse farm used to school young horses). Each of these facilities charges a standard day rate that includes housing, food, and personal care. It does not include veterinary fees and services such as shoeing, which must be done by a professional farrier (blacksmith). While being trained at the track, a horse will need to be shod more frequently and see a vet more often as its training regimen becomes more intense. Figure in an additional hundred to three hundred dollars per month for those vet and farrier bills, on top of the higher day rate at the track.

As stated earlier, the current day rate at a racetrack in the larger racing cities runs from about $55 to $75 per day. On a horse farm, however, $25 to $35 a day is more likely. And at a training facility, the price will settle somewhere in the middle.

Unexpected costs will also arise. Set aside money in case your horse gets sick, suffers an accident, fractures a bone, or needs extended training time.

Periodic costs must also be anticipated. Once the horse starts racing, bonuses must be paid to both the trainer and jockey each time the horse finishes "in the money." This will, of course, reduce the net amount of the winnings. There are also fees for nominations and entering certain races, as well as transportation costs. With all these expenses, you can see the advantage to owning horses in partnership.

Consider how much you can afford, figuring in the monthly maintenance costs and periodic costs. If you find a horse or partnership you like but can't afford, don't get in beyond your means. There are many partnerships available at every financial level. You will enjoy a safer and more satisfying outcome if you take the time and effort to shop around and find the deal that best fits you.

Some racing fans have gotten their feet wet by dabbling with fantastically low-cost offerings. One survey turned up a group proffering a share for $350. Another partnership, available through the Internet, would let people in at $100 increments. Activity at this level affords little involvement, yet such offerings do exist.

Owning even a very small percentage of a racehorse excites some people as much as betting at the track. It doesn't require a lot of out-of-pocket expense and yet they feel involved. The down side is that participants don't feel especially connected to their horse or to one another, as the managing partner finds it almost impossible to communicate constantly with such a large group of investors.

Consider this: If someone puts together a partnership for a $50,000 horse that will cost $18,000 a year to maintain, the total needed for the first year is $68,000. At the minimum rate of a hundred dollars per investor, there could be as many as 680 partners! Some people will put in more than the minimum, but even if the average were $500 per investor, there would still be 136 partners. As it is, every manager struggles to find time to keep partners informed of the progress of their horses, respond to questions, and answer mail. How could any manager maintain a relationship with that many people? Although some people may be content to track their horses by reading updates on the Internet, others prefer something more tangible.

If a managing partner deals with no more than twenty people, the partnership is more reasonable to manage. Furthermore, when each person contributes a sizeable investment, he or she tends to remain a long-term partner.

To get into a partnership with reasonable involvement, you should plan to invest between five thousand and ten thousand dollars. See the following chart for an illustration of the benefits of sharing costs and of diversification.

Investors with more money can afford horses that sell at auctions for between $50,000 and $100,000. Partnerships involving horses in this range usually have three to five investors and require an outlay of $50,000 or more.

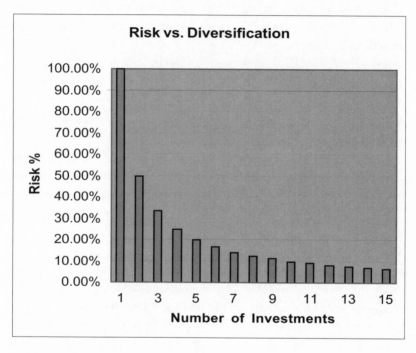

High rollers are often not interested in owning horses in partnership. They are likely to prefer setting up a personal stable of horses. They may make an exception when a potentially popular stallion is syndicated and buy a share for hundreds of thousands of dollars.

Rich or not, we all have the same objective: find a bargain. That is, buy low and sell high. We have all been cautioned, "You only get what you pay for." This, however, is not always true. Take the champion Real Quiet for example. Purchased for $17,000, this Kentucky Derby winner ended up winning more than $3 million over a couple of years. No one finds that kind of a deal on a regular basis, but keep looking. Seek out partners with an ability to rec-

RICK SAMUELS

Real Quiet — one of racing's great bargains.

ognize that diamond in the rough. If you can purchase a horse at a bargain price, you may stand in the winner's circle accumulating profits.

Diversification

You diversify when you make sure all your eggs aren't in a single basket. You can diversify in the horse business by owning more than one horse within a partnership, having an interest in more than one type of partnership, or by participating in a partnership with more than one objective. For example, a partnership might own two horses: one for racing and the other for a quick resale, called pinhooking. If the racehorse doesn't prove successful, the second horse may make up for the loss if it sells for a high price.

When you diversify, you lessen the risk and increase the odds of making a profit. With a partnership you may own only 5, 10, or 25 percent of the holdings, but when you split your investment into different categories or several horses, your chances of success multiply.

The typical horses sold at auction range between $5,000 and $50,000. It's here that partnerships provide marvelous relief. By sharing the cost, a partnership may buy into two or more horses and give the group a better chance of picking a winner. Sharing costs may also allow you to participate in more than one partnership.

Putting all of your money into one horse becomes a total win-or-lose proposition. Owning a smaller percentage, either by investing in two or three horses in one partnership or by investing in more than one partnership, creates a much better chance of turning a profit. Although all three horses aren't likely to be winners, neither are they all likely to be losers. If at least one of the three is outstanding, it can make up for the expense of the entire group.

Professional Management

All partnerships, no matter how they are legally and financially configured, have a managing partner who oversees the objectives of the group. This is especially advantageous when you are just getting started.

You need a managing partner for two reasons. First, you'll want someone who is willing to take responsibility and legal liability of the enterprise. Secondly, you'll need a professional who knows the business well enough to make informed decisions about your horse, where it should compete, what it may need for care or training, and so on.

For these reasons, the managing partner usually will be either a trainer or a breeder.

The Satisfaction of Sharing

Whenever an event involving your partnership's horse or horses occurs, those investors who can free up their time are likely to attend. Maybe it's a race; maybe it's an auction; or maybe it's a visit to the farm to watch a foal being born. You may be lucky enough at one of these events or over time to find someone that you really connect with in your group. It's fun to have a partner you like to call, join for dinner, or go with to the races or horse farms. But even without such a special friend, each of these experiences will be interesting and exciting. Cot Campbell, who owns Dogwood Stable in South Carolina and has sold partnership interests in racehorses for decades, has this to say in his book *Lightning in a Jar* (Eclipse Press 2000): "This is supposed to be fun! You would like to make money. Sure! And you want to be able to write off your losses if you don't. But the most important consideration is that this venture is supposed to put a little zest in your life. Fun is what it's all about!

"So, make sure the chemistry is right when you make a connection. Hook up with people you like because life's too short — and this game has too many downs between the ups — not to make the journey with someone you're fond of."

Wealthy people who are committed to building a stable of horses may find that owning horses individually is most satisfying. For the majority of us, however, the tremendous benefit derived from dividing the costs of an expensive operation, having a professional manage our enterprise, mitigating the risk through diversification without having to double or triple the outlay of cash, and sharing our efforts and the joy of our successes with other dedicated people can't be beat.

The Four Types of Partnerships

The Thoroughbred industry is much more vast than most people realize. Billions of dollars and hundreds of thousands of people are dedicated to making racing a worldwide competition. Consequently, there are many ways to get involved.

For our purposes the industry can be divided into four basic areas: racing, claiming, pinhooking, and breeding. Each has its own type of excitement and level of risk. For instance, buying into a breeding partnership exposes the owner to lower risk but provides less action. Racing and claiming are faster paced and exciting but come with higher risk and more costly maintenance fees. The following definitions will help sketch out the larger picture and will be followed with more detailed information in the next chapter on how partnerships operate in each of these areas.

Racing

Racing partnerships serve those who intend to race a horse for as long as it is profitable to do so. A horse the partnership purchases with this intent may be so young as not to be ready to race just yet and will have to go through training. On the other hand, there are always horses currently competing that are for sale so the partners can enjoy more immediate action.

In order to compete, all horses must be placed with a licensed, professional trainer. Often, the trainer acts as the managing partner of a racing partnership. Owners/partners may visit their horses on the backside of the track, discuss strategy with the trainer, and talk to the jockeys before the race.

Claiming

Another way for partners to get into the action almost immediately is to form a claiming partnership. When someone "claims" a horse, it means he or she has purchased it at a racetrack out of a claiming race. The majority of races contested at any track are claiming races. To run a horse in a claiming race, owners must be willing to sell their charge to any buyer who puts up the claiming fee before the race begins. The claiming price is stated at the top of the daily program with the other conditions of the race.

Horses in claiming races may be acquired by depositing the purchase price at the track office at least fifteen minutes before the race starts (some restrictions apply; see chapter 3, "Claiming Partnerships"). The horse becomes the property of the new owner the moment the starting gate opens, but the previous owner gets any of the purse money won in that race. Insurance is available to protect the owners against the horse having an accident during that particular race. This will also be discussed in more detail under the section dealing with claiming partnerships.

The new owner must have a trainer registered at that track who will take possession of the horse immediately after the race. Often, trainers also act as the managing partner of a claiming partnership.

Claiming is a fast business. A person can go to the track on any given day and become a racehorse owner. Although a few restrictions apply, and will be discussed in the next chapter, claiming partnerships can be formed to acquire horses that race for modest or expensive purses.

Pinhooking

Pinhooking refers to buying a young horse with the intent of making a profit by reselling it a short time later, usually within six months. Pinhooking partnerships often use horse farm owners, trainers, or bloodstock agents as their managing partners.

An investor may buy a young horse at a sale or auction in the fall and sell it in the spring of the following year. Pinhooking works because a horse matures very quickly during the first two years of its life. It requires a keen eye and a lot of experience to identify which of these gawky young animals will fill out and develop the physique of an athlete within that period. When the buyer's instinct proves correct and the horse develops nicely, an immediate profit results. By making the right selection, and if Lady Luck helps things along, the buyer can realize a several hundred percent profit.

Breeding

Every year horse farms provide the racing industry with a new batch of foals by mating horses that have complementary strengths in their pedigrees. In a breeding partnership, a horse farm owner is usually selected as the managing partner, and you own a share or percentage of a stallion, a broodmare, or a foal. Horse farms abound in every state from California to Maryland, with a large concentration in Kentucky. Almost without exception, any horse farm in your state would welcome your involvement.

Finding Your Fit

So before you enter into a partnership offering, consider the benefits and experiences of each type. It may be that a friend has invited you to join a partnership in which she is involved. Even if it wouldn't be your first choice, you might want to consider it just for the fun of teaming up with her and getting your feet wet in the industry through her knowledge and experience.

If, on the other hand, you don't have such a friend but just love the horses and the environment surrounding them, consider first your own personality and what type of partnership you think would be most thrilling. There is every bit as much thrill in watching a foal come into the world as there is in watching a competitor cross the finish line first. Finding where you best fit will go a long way toward providing the fulfillment you'd like to have from your investment.

In the next chapter, we will also highlight those things that make each partnership type uniquely rewarding.

Identify Personal Goals

Although all of us love horses, our goals may differ. Consider the following possibilities and list them according to your priorities. Then think for a minute. Are there any other things that would be important for you? If so, make a note of them.

- Be near to, and spend as much time with, the horses as possible.
- Watch your horses compete in races.
- Begin a family, or stable, of horses.
- Make a profit.
- Manage the career of your horses by acting as the managing partner.
- Search for the "big horse" that could take you to the Kentucky Derby or other large stakes race.

Once you have identified a few basic goals, your selection of the right kind of partnership will be much easier. Then you must give realistic thought to those things that might limit your involvement, or modify your goals.

Accept Your Limitations

Although any number of factors could come into play, the two areas most likely to curb your involvement (other than money) are time and travel.

Time

If you are already busy with work, family, and other commitments, limit your involvement by cherry-picking those activities that will bring you the most enjoyment. For instance, you may want to visit the horse farm while on a vacation with your family. If racing is your game, you may limit your attendance only to when your horses are running at a track near you. Follow their progress the rest of the time on the Internet. You can vary these ideas, but the key is to make choices that fit your lifestyle.

Maybe you are retired or have a lot of flextime. If you also have extra funds at your disposal, what a lucky person you are! Your racing interest can now open worlds of experience to you that very few people will ever have a chance to enjoy. You may decide to get involved with racing and breeding partnerships. You may want to learn enough that you can put together your own partnerships and act as the managing partner, working directly with the trainers, horse farms, and other professionals. Think of the possibilities!

For the first couple of years, you may want to be a quiet partner and just watch how things operate. Like most everything, however, you will get out what you put in. The more involved and knowledgeable you become about your horses and what's happening to them, the more enjoyment you will derive. Also, the more you pay attention to the business aspect, the more likely it is that you will make a profit.

Some people experience the typical pattern of becoming enthused and involved at the beginning and then gradually backing off. Try not to let this happen. Life can get hectic, so assign your horse business a certain priority and a scheduled amount of time.

One tool to use that will help keep the enthusiasm vibrant is *The Blood-Horse*. This weekly news magazine comes as part of your membership to the Thoroughbred Owners and Breeders Association. This not-for-profit organization in Lexington, Kentucky, produces a number of publications, seminars, organized tours, and other events to inform and educate owners.

When your local track is holding its race meet, you may want to go one day a week. You will certainly want to be there to watch your horse run, but make it a point to spend some time on the backside also. When you go, don't just visit with your trainer for an hour, watch your horse work out, and then go home. Rather, spend an additional couple of hours visiting with exercise riders and jockeys, hanging out at the cafeteria, and giving yourself an opportunity to learn from other people. Put it on your calendar as an appointment. If you wait until you just "have some extra time," it's not likely that you will be there often enough.

If you are involved in a breeding partnership, talk to the horse farm manager about the best times to visit during the year. If you own a stallion or broodmare, you may want to watch the breeding process, be present at the foaling, meet a vet, or watch any number of activities at a farm.

As stated earlier, if you are at a time in your life when you simply can't put in much time, a partnership will get you into the game and provide an education in this sport. As time goes by, though, plan to increase your involvement and take advantage of all the opportunities you can.

The Thoroughbred Owners and Breeders Association, Thoroughbred Owners of California, and individual tracks put on wonderful seminars. Videotapes also are available that explain how trainers work, how to evaluate the conformation of a horse, how to understand the pedigree lines of a horse, and the list goes on. Look under the Resources section at the back of this book for a list of places you can shop for these materials.

Travel

Those people who have discretionary income and time to go along with it can enjoy their ownership with a great deal of latitude. The only real limit is their desire or energy level. Others, however, must think about financial restrictions.

It may be wise to select a partnership that lets you remain within your budget. Even though you'd prefer the racing aspect, maybe you don't have a track close enough for you to attend without requiring travel and the consequent expense. You may love the idea of pinhooking but live too far from the sales facilities to enjoy the action up close. In these situations it may be better to connect with a local partnership that has events you can get to and enjoy without requiring a big outlay of extra cash.

Those who can afford and enjoy traveling may select partnerships in cities they love to visit or in locations where they have a second home. Still others may look at the various tracks the horses move to throughout the year (known as a circuit) and select a partnership in that area so they can enjoy each location on the circuit.

When you talk with a trainer, ask what circuit he or she follows. A trainer from Louisiana may race his horses at Fair Grounds Race Course in New Orleans, then move to Lone Star Park in Dallas, and finally into Kentucky. That's a lot of ground to cover, but the trainer must keep his horses active all year long. In the more populated areas like south Florida, New York, and Los Angeles, the trainer may be able to stable his horses at one location and van them to whatever track is currently conducting its meet. This is certainly an easier life for the trainer, and for the horses, too. Those trainers who must relocate at longer distances must have auxiliary housing and be willing to spend a lot of time away from their families. That can be a tough life. But for your purposes, traveling occasionally to see your horses at various points on their circuit can be fun.

When preparing for a trip, logon to www.bloodhorse.com, and you can also find a complete list of all upcoming auctions. If you can, schedule enough time to attend. You'll learn a great deal.

The same goes for visiting any of the big horse farms, particularly if you can get to Kentucky. Just go through the ads in *The Blood-Horse* magazine and pick out two or three of the ones you'd like to visit. Call and set up an appointment, and you'll have a very memorable time while increasing your education.

And speaking of Kentucky, if you ever get a chance to go there, make every effort to visit the Kentucky Horse Park in Lexington. You will step right up close to retired but famous racehorses such as Cigar and John Henry, learn about the many breeds of horses, enjoy topnotch entertainment, and have research available on almost every topic you can think of in the all-inclusive library.

Do you enjoy international travel? Racing is big in Australia, Brazil, England, France, Germany, Ireland, Japan, and United Arab Emirates. For a list of international tracks, visit the International Racing Bureau's web site: irbracing.com.

So if you have the time and wherewithal to travel, you will find many ways to enjoy your ownership. If, on the other hand, you have to limit your travel, you can still enjoy a fulfilling experience by getting those things you can participate in on your schedule.

All of us live with restrictions. Look at the positive side instead of thinking of such limitations as confining. We should understand that those parameters outline an area within which we are free to enjoy ourselves. We can romp and jump and frolic to our heart's content within those boundaries and relax knowing that we play within a field that is safe from harm.

To sum up, maybe you never thought you could own a racehorse. But now that so many partnerships offer a sharing of costs, professional management, and diversification for only a fraction of the total investment, the fantasy becomes within reach. Taking into consideration both your goals and limitations, it now becomes important to match your personality with the type of partnership that is likely to bring you the most pleasure and reward.

In the next chapter, we will discuss why some people find a better fit in a particular type of partnership rather than another. See if you can discover the one that best fits your personality.

3

Understanding Types of Partnerships

I t is possible to categorize partnerships in any number of ways. For example, partnerships can be grouped depending on how much it costs to get in on the action or on how many partners are involved. Still others can be categorized by their legal structure: general partnerships, limited partnerships, limited liability companies, and so on.

For our purposes partnerships have been divided into four types of involvement: breeding, pinhooking, racing, and claiming. They appear in this order based on the speed of the action, going from the slowest to the fastest, with the understanding that the faster the action, the faster the money may go out the door.

Breeding Partnerships

Breeding partnerships sell a percentage of ownership in a broodmare. (Stallion syndications are also considered breeding partnerships and will be covered at the end of the chapter.) When you become a member of a breeding partnership, you are signing up for the purchase and maintenance of a filly or mare that may or may not be pregnant. As your goal is to see this mare produce athletes that can win lucrative stakes races, you and your partners will want to invest in a mare that has three qualifications: an excellent pedigree, or parentage; a balanced and strong conformation, or build; and a winning record that gives evidence she was a better-than-average athlete.

The least risky way for a partnership to acquire such an animal is to purchase one that has already produced one or more stakes-winning progeny; it's a good bet that she will produce more. Of course, she'll be more expensive than an unproven mare.

These proven producers will, of necessity, be older mares. The time it takes them to acquire these credentials adds up. She will probably race until she is a four-year-old, and then when she is bred, it will be another year before the foal is born, and another two before that foal is of racing age. The mare probably will be about eight or nine years old by the time her first offspring proves itself on the track. These older broodmares can still be a good deal as their fertility can last into their early twenties.

Most people who form breeding partnerships go the less expensive way and buy a filly or mare that has proven herself in every other way except as a broodmare. She may still be racing, or she may be offered at auction already impregnated by a reputable stallion. After the birth of the first foal, of course, your partnership will have the discretion of selecting her next mate. This is a very important decision, and the partnership will want expert advice before contracting for the right to breed her to a given stallion.

Consider that a stallion will cover, or mate with, many mares during a breeding season and may produce thousands of foals in his lifetime. Only a small percentage of those foals will become stakes winners, but when they do, it causes his stud fee to go up. The more highly ranked the stakes race, and the higher the purse money, the more rapidly his stud fee will increase. Besides this, his "book" (a schedule of commitments to breed with mares) will stay full. If he can now cover twice as many mares and at a much larger fee, it is easy to see how his owners can profit.

For example, Storm Cat's stud fee started at $20,000 in 1991 and is now $500,000 because of his success as a sire. As of the end of 2002, he had sired 106 stakes winners, the most notable of which are Giant's Causeway and Cat Thief.

In contrast, a mare can only produce one foal per year. If two or three of her foals turn out to be stakes winners, every new foal she produces will bring a premium price.

When horses are sold at auction, each horse's parentage and history are summarized on a single catalog page. The display of the paternal side will only list the sire's heritage. On the maternal side, however, the parentage is detailed for two to three generations back. (A detailed explanation and samples of a catalog page are found in chapter 11.) Opinions differ on whether the sire or the dam is more influential in producing successful runners. Obviously, both are important.

As you consider the risk and reward of investing in broodmares, you'll want one whose foals can be sold for enough money that after two years you're "out" of her. That is, the income from the sale of those first two foals will completely cover the costs of her purchase and upkeep. If you can do that, the rest is gravy.

Here is another rule of thumb: When choosing a stallion to mate with a broodmare, the stud fee should not exceed one-fourth the cost of the mare. For example, a $40,000 broodmare would merit a stallion with a $10,000 stud fee. If you get those numbers too out of whack, you end up with so much invested that you can't get out safely and need something big to recoup. That isn't smart, so be careful and discuss it with your partners.

The people who most enjoy breeding partnerships tend to be those in love with the animals. They like the care, feeding, and nurturing of an animal and its offspring. This kind of investment does not carry the fast-paced thrill of a racing partnership. A mare will give birth to a foal just once a year, in the spring. Although she will be bred again as soon as possible, it is another year of waiting for the next birth.

ANNE M. EBERHARDT

Breeding partnerships can take longer to yield results.

Although breeding partnerships are by nature slower paced, think of the advantages. You can get in for less money, you don't have to pay as high maintenance fees as in the other types of partnerships, you can visit the horse farm and observe the breeding and foaling process, and you also have a growing inventory of new stock that you can choose to sell or race. Although not carrying the excitement of having a horse in a race every few weeks, breeding partnerships are the only ones that come close to guaranteeing a revenue stream. For many people, that slower pace provides an ideal way to get into this game with some degree of confidence.

With luck, these owners see a foal born every year. Then they watch it develop and grow. As the foal matures, the partners decide if they want to sell it at some point or keep it for racing. In either case, they enjoy the excitement of following each youngster as it achieves new levels of success, even if they no longer own it. It's like watching your own children excel. Every time an individual from your family of horses runs or is sold for a higher price, you will take pride in its achievement. Of course, now that you are no

A breeding partnership can see a foal born each year.

longer the owner of that horse but only the owner of its parents, you will not be invited into the winner's circle. But you will cheer just as loudly when you see that youngster run.

Furthermore, the emotional thrill is not the only benefit. Every time an off-spring from your broodmare moves up a level at an auction, or wins a race, or produces a new winner, it immediately affects your bottom line. The stud fee for the stallion goes up, and the price of the next foal coming out of the broodmare also goes up. Sometimes, the price increases several times over. If two or three offspring of your broodmare win stakes races, the market for foals out of your mare will skyrocket. And that is where the profits lie.

Finally, think of how fast your family of young horses can grow. If your breeding partnership involves the ownership of two or more broodmares, you will now have at least two families of offspring to follow. In just a few years, you will be keeping track of quite a number of horses. Following their careers can become a fascinating hobby. You will find it is easy to track each of the horses in your "family" using the Internet. For instance, the *Daily Racing Form* at www.drf.com has a free service called "Watches" that will alert you any time your horses post formal workouts or are entered into races. You could also establish a "Virtual Stable" at www.equibase.com to accomplish much the same thing. Numerous other services are available and are listed in the Resources section at the back of this book. Check them out to find the ones you prefer. No matter which ones you select, if you set up a horse watch or virtual stable you'll be alerted automatically. The action may be slower than racing, but the thrills and satisfaction are unmatched.

Pinhooking Partnerships

Here lies an interesting adventure for the stouthearted investor. Pinhooking, as explained in chapter two, is buying a young horse with the intent of selling it for a higher price, normally within a matter of months. Some people are in this game more for turning a profit than for the sport of racing. No problem with that. Most of us want to profit, and as large amounts of money pass hands in the buying and selling of Thoroughbreds, pinhooking offers a good venue for such an enterprise.

The average price of a yearling sold at auction in 2002 was $43,699 while the median (or middle point) was $11,000. Many of these young horses end up selling for $250,000 and some into the millions. For pinhookers who can spot those young horses that may experience extraordinary physical development within the next few months, the spread (or difference between the purchase and sale price) is a good one.

Some find pinhooking distasteful. They look at those who deal in horseflesh with no intention of racing the animals as being less than sportsmen. Nevertheless, many good horsemen have made pinhooking their specialty because of the significant and relatively quick income. They find little difference in what they do when compared to any other business that an owner may love and that also produces a profit.

If you like the idea of pinhooking, there are partnerships restricted to this effort. The majority of those who pinhook, however, are also involved in racing. As owners, trainers, and bloodstock agents buy and sell horses year after year, some develop an eye keen enough to spot a pinhooking opportunity and jump on it.

You may even find an occasional pinhooking opportunity offered in a larger partnership deal. For example, a partnership may purchase more than one horse with the intent of racing one horse and pinhooking the others. This provides another opportunity of spreading risk. If one side of the partnership isn't successful, maybe the other will make up for the loss.

This is precisely what happened in one of my partnerships. A group of us bought into a partnership that contained two horses, both of them yearlings. The plan was to keep one for racing and pinhook the other. As it turned out, the filly we bought for racing grew big and looked beautiful but didn't seem to have the heart for racing. After more than a year of working with her, the group decided to sell her. However, we acquired the other filly for $45,000 and sold her at auction four months later for $200,000. Although we lost money on the racing filly, we made an overall profit from the pinhooking side. Diversifying our interest within the partnership gave us more than one chance to make a profit.

Candidates for pinhooking are usually bought at auctions, but many are purchased privately from breeding farms. Horse farms, trainers, and bloodstock agents (who are experts at understanding bloodlines and value) put together this type of partnership. They attend several auctions every year and maintain a relationship with owners who are willing to sell privately. They are continually on the lookout for opportunities.

If you are interested in pinhooking and have a relationship with any of these professionals, talk to them about your interest. First find out how much experience that particular person has had with pinhooking and his measure of success. Then see if he knows of others who might join with you in forming a partnership the next time he finds a good possibility. Pinhooking partnerships can be put together quickly if the managing partner knows of an interested party ahead of time.

The thrill of pinhooking is akin to the excitement of shopping or bargain hunting. If you love to find a good deal, you'll love pinhooking. The thrill that belongs to the treasure hunters, whether they discover their prize at a luxury department store, a flea market, an antique shop, or an auction barn,

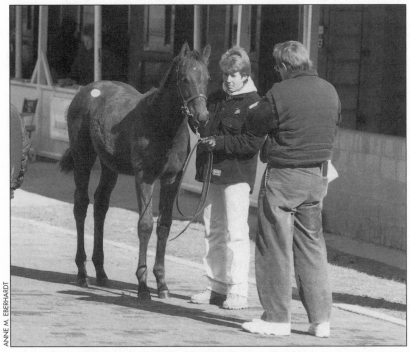

Weanlings are frequently purchased as pinhooking prospects.

is akin to winning the lottery. All players put on poker faces and act non-chalant until the auctioneer's gavel declares the new owner. Then it's a no-holds-barred celebration with merriment to bask in for a long time. Successful pinhookers tell eye-popping stories of big profits made in a short while. Naturally, those who walk away bruised aren't so quick to share their stories, but they will never stop looking.

The action in pinhooking is somewhat faster than that in breeding but not as fast as in racing. It's even a little slower yet if you pinhook through a partnership than if you have adequate funds to do it on your own. The difference is the time it takes to get the investors together and to prepare the partnership agreement.

An additional advantage is that pinhooking involves the partners for the shortest duration. Most pinhooking endeavors are completed within six months. A disadvantage, for some, is the lack of emotional connection to the horse. It is no more than a commodity ventured in for profit.

If you'd like to give pinhooking a try, you may want to put together the investors and the agreement first. The benefit of having the people and the money ready to go is that when your managing partner or agent finds a good deal, he or she can act on it right away. The hazard of this approach is that with money already at hand, it's easy to grab at what appears to be the best deal but may not represent a genuine discovery of value.

Almost as soon as you acquire your new bargain, you'll begin to prepare it for the sale. It may need to be fattened up, taught how to stand and hold itself, and trained to show itself in the best possible light. The costs of having this work done is on par with having a horse at a training facility; that is, somewhere between the high costs of having a horse racing at a track and the lower costs of having it kept on a farm. The cost will also vary depending on the locale of the facility. Finally, the day of the auction arrives. As the bidding takes place, you'll find yourself holding your breath. Will others see the value you have seen? You may undergo the humiliation of having no one bid anywhere close to what you expected. Or you may also cry out with joy as the price zooms beyond your expectations. Just talk to those involved in pinhooking, and they'll soon have you fired up with how exciting and profitable it can be.

The Blood-Horse reported in 2002 that the rate of return on pinhooking had hit new levels. Yearlings pinhooked in the up to $19,999 price range during 2002 were the most likely to bring a profit (an average 168 percent rate of return). Next were those yearlings pinhooked in the $20,000 to $29,999 range (also an average 168 percent rate of return). Pretty darned impressive. But wait! You must also realize that only 48 percent of those that ventured into this arena had any increase at all. Many who had purchased the more expensive youngsters decided not to let them go for either a wash or a loss and kept them to race. It's important to look at both sides of this picture before you get involved.

You bought this bargain to try and turn it quickly into a significant profit. And you can play this game repeatedly, providing you have the financial capacity, the market stays favorable, and you make the right choices. A good number of people, after all, make their living doing just that. It's relatively fast action that offers both high risk and high reward. Maybe that's the game for you.

Racing Partnerships

The action gets significantly faster here. It may start out a bit slow, but once your animals are healthy and at the track, racing will keep you busy.

A racing partnership consists of purchasing horses that either are in training to race or are currently racing. Most partnership offerings begin with two-year-olds that are about to begin their career. Other partnerships, however, are designed to acquire horses three or more years old that show a lot of promise.

A horse may become the property of a succession of owners. The previous owner may feel that the horse has not shown much promise, doesn't appear to have a heart for racing, or may have a tendency to sickness or injury. The new owner, on the other hand, may believe that the horse has not been trained effectively, has been raced above its level, or maybe has been raced in the wrong part of the country. For instance, southern California tracks offer larger purses and are considered among the most competitive places for horses to race. A partnership may be formed to buy one or more horses currently running in southern California that have shown real promise but have not yet been able to beat the field in that locale. The plan is to send the new acquisition to northern California, or to another part of the country, where it will stand a greater chance of capturing the winning purse among horses of a lower class.

It has been said that all matters in the racing business are measured at the track. But the track is also the arena that exposes the horse and its owner to the highest risk. The costs represented by the day rate, farrier bills, medical expenses, and so on are much higher here. And, of course, the risk of injury increases as the horse pushes itself to new levels. When you add that less than half of horses that compete will become winners, things start sounding pretty glum. Still, many insist, "Baby, this is where the action is."

Once a horse is healthy and in top form, it is always getting ready for the next race. Depending on the individual horse, it may be raced every two or three weeks. Some horses need a longer rest to regain the stamina necessary for their next effort. At this stage your trainer is scanning the condition book (a track publication that lists upcoming races), looking for a race that fits your horse. If you stay involved with your racing stock, this will be a busy time for you as well. And that is especially true if you plan to attend each time your horses race.

In a racing partnership, the action not only is fast but also loaded with emotional highs and lows. It helps a lot if you have a partnership that owns more than one horse. Maybe one will win and the other will not. One may come close but be disqualified for bumping into another horse. Each time an incident like that happens, your stomach will turn inside out. You'll carry that sunken feeling for days. In contrast, when the color of the silks that cross that finish line first belongs to you, it will be difficult to remain calm. Ecstasy at its best! A day at the track when your horse is running may blow you high or low, but it will always be a day you won't forget.

Most people involved in racing are looking for that roller-coaster ride. When your name is tied to a particular horse, the thrill is akin to having run the race yourself. Whatever happens to that horse happens to you. You may find yourself feeling edgy and impatient when something slows down training between races. That edginess, however, will vanish like a cloud on a windy day when your horse is entered into its next competition.

You'll be packing up for the track to see just how brightly the sun will shine on you that day.

Claiming Partnerships

Thoroughbreds compete in three categories of races: claiming, allowance, and handicap. Each category allows horses of similar ability to compete. (For an explanation of each type of race and how they differ, see Appendix A.) Horses that race in the claiming category provide a unique business opportunity that does not exist in the allowance and handicap categories.

More than 70 percent of all races run in the United States are claiming races. To enter a horse in this type of race, the owner takes the chance, or opportunity, of having his horse bought, or "claimed," at the stated claiming price. The prospective owner must be licensed with the state and have a trainer working at that track ready to receive the horse into his barn.

The purpose of the claiming race is to level the field, allowing the majority of horses an opportunity to race against those of similar caliber. An intelligent owner of a really strong horse would not risk losing his horse in a claiming race where it clearly outclassed the others, just for that day's purse money. This deterrent forces owners to race their animals in like company. If there were no way to compel them to do so, only the best horses would win every race. Not much fun in that. The claiming race also provides an entry-level opportunity for horses that have not yet proven to their owners that they can, in fact, win. Horses entered in these races are not expected to compete in the more difficult handicap or even allowance races, at least not yet.

Claiming can bring quick results.

To claim a horse out of a race, the prospective owner, or managing partner of a group, will either establish a financial account or deposit a cashier's check with the paymaster of the track. He will then fill out an "agreement to claim" card and deposit it in the claim-card box at least fifteen minutes before the race begins. If he is the only person to file a claim, he will own the horse from the moment the starting gate opens. If more than one person submits a claim, the new owner will be determined by lot after the race. One strange aspect of this procedure is that the new owner is responsible for that horse, and any problems it may have, even during that race. On the other hand, if any purse money is won, it goes to the previous owner. After waiting at least two weeks, the new owner can begin racing the horse under new colors as long as it races for a 25 percent higher claiming price. Otherwise, a thirty-day wait is commonly required. The wait varies from track to track, but owners and trainers still refer to it as having their horse "in jail."

When a horse wins a claiming race, the owners will race it in higher-level claiming races, and this can continue indefinitely. Obviously, if it shows exceptional speed or has won two or more races in a row, the probability of its being claimed rises in a hurry. To prevent this, the owner will move it to

Entering a claim in the claim box.

the more lucrative and protected allowance level.

Claiming is one of the least expensive ways of obtaining a racehorse. The time spent teaching the animal the basics and getting it in shape have already been invested. The day rates and other costs of bringing it to the level of competition have been spent. There it stands, ready to go. You immediately have a contender.

But what if it turns out that something is wrong with the horse? When you claim a horse, you get it as-is. So "buyers beware." There is no guarantee or return policy. After all, another reason horses are put into claiming races is to get rid of them. This is why it will be imperative for you to find a trainer who specializes in claiming horses.

Actively buying and selling in the claiming business requires a lot of focus. There are trainers who will proclaim that they can put together a breeding partnership, a pinhooking partnership, and are ready to claim whenever you say so. Be cautious about the person who tells you he is a jack-of-all-trades; he may also be the master of none.

Although every trainer is licensed to do all those things, if you'd like to focus on one area, find someone who specializes in it. A trainer who concentrates on claiming will watch for prospective claimers at all times. If he knows you are interested in claiming at a certain price level, he not only will be familiar with a number of horses that would serve as candidates but will also know other professionals at the track whose opinions he can solicit before narrowing the choice to one or two. And what may be most important, he will keep his eye on that prospect, watching for any flaw, right up to the last minute when you drop your application to claim into the box.

The people who love this type of partnership are not trying to claim a horse they hope will turn into a Kentucky Derby winner. Indeed, horses have become champions from the claiming ranks, but it is unusual. Those who claim horses enjoy the fast action. They claim horses and put them back at risk all the time. The appeal of claiming partnerships is that they marry the desire to race and the desire to find a good bargain. These are the people who get the thrill of owning a horse that may win races but may also be claimed at a higher price. Along with the higher risk comes the higher reward.

Those who want into the horse game right now, with lots of action, will find nothing better or faster than claiming a horse. All of the action described under racing partnerships is also true for claiming partnerships with an additional benefit: on any given day, you can go home with a horse that is ready to run.

Stallion Syndications

An additional way to participate in a breeding partnership is to purchase one or more shares in a stallion that has been syndicated. As it belongs in the category of breeding partnerships, stallion syndication merits mention, but it usually requires a great deal more capital than is available to someone who wants to own a Thoroughbred "without spending a fortune."

In the Thoroughbred business, a stallion is a male horse that has been "put to stud." That is, he will be used to sire an entire new generation of offspring that will hopefully inherit many of his genetic and winning charac-

Owning a piece of a stallion can require a big investment.

42

teristics. As was mentioned earlier, a stallion can be very prolific. It is common these days for a popular stallion to sire seventy-five to one hundred new foals each year. The impact on the industry is considerable.

A stallion earns money for its owners primarily from the stud fee charged for covering (or impregnating) a mare — the more successful the stallion, the higher the fee. Stud fees begin at about $1,000 and have climbed to the astronomical height of more than $700,000. Most fees, though, range from $5,000 to $20,000. The stallion Storm Cat currently stands at the top of the heap by commanding $500,000 per mating! Now that, as they say, is a lot of hay.

Even at $5,000, if a stallion covers seventy-five mares in a season, he will produce an annual income of $375,000. Consequently, many horses that are retired to stud are worth millions of dollars. Through syndication, the risks/rewards are shared.

Most original owners keep the right to breed the stallion to a mare once each year. Cot Campbell gives the best explanation in his book *Lightning in a Jar*: "The difference between a share and a breeding right is that a share is a unit of ownership. It is negotiable. It can be bought or sold. A breeding right is the expense-free right to breed a mare to that stallion annually. That right cannot be sold. For instance, you can sell your 1999 season to the stallion for the published stud fee, or for whatever you can get; but you cannot sell the lifetime breeding right. You — the owner — must utilize it in some way on an annual basis: breed on it, or sell the stud season annually. But the 'right' cannot be sold on the open market as you would a share in a stock (or a syndicate share). And, usually, it's renewable each year at the pleasure of the syndicate. Should it become necessary — because of age, for instance — to reduce the 'book' of the stallion (the number of mares he can service), breeding rights are the first to go."

The horse farm at which the stallion will stand will be given a number of seasons in exchange for caring for the animal and overseeing its breeding career. The remaining seasons will be sold or contracted out. Although each owner can decide how many shares will comprise the syndicate, forty shares are customary. Owner of the shares may breed their own mares to the stallion or may sell the right. Due to the high cost of acquiring a stallion season, few novice horsemen get started at this level. A more common way for a beginner to end up owning a stallion season is to grow into it.

Say, for instance, you bought a percentage of a broodmare that then gave birth to a colt. The partners decided to race him, and he turned out to be exceptional, winning a number of graded stakes races and a significant amount of money. That horse would be a good candidate to become a stallion, and the managing partner might then suggest syndicating the horse.

There are several benefits. First, the original partners receive a nice infusion of cash and a good return on investment right away through the sale of the shares. They also retain ownership of a number of stallion seasons. If the horse's progeny start winning stakes races, the stud fee goes up. If the partners also own broodmares, they can use their shares for mating with the stallion without additional cost and then sell any remaining seasons, providing a revenue stream for the partnership. Owning a successful sire can make you a lot of money.

Of course, the converse is also true. If the stallion's progeny don't win races, the value of the stud fee will drop like stock after a bad earnings report. Not only will those who bought stallion shares at the time of syndication not make money, they could stand to lose their investment if the stallion's book cannot be filled. This problem, however, doesn't represent the same risk for the original owners. Whether or not the offspring do well, they will have already made a profit by having created the syndication and having sold the seasons to the new investors.

So, there are the five types of partnerships. Did you find one or more of them that seem to match your personality and interest? Over time, you may find more than one aspect of this sport that attracts you. Involvement in one area often opens the door to trying something else with partners you've met or done business with before. That's part of the fun.

As you investigate partnerships offered to the public, you may come across a few people who use different terms than have been used here. That's fine; let those making the offer define exactly what they have on hand. Regardless of the words used, however, you will have the best experience possible if you can match the excitement you seek, the risk you can tolerate, and the speed of the action with the types of partnerships being offered.

4

Where to Find Partnership Offerings

I t is possible to start your own partnership with interested friends and others. How to do so will be covered at the end of this chapter. For your initial foray, however, you will probably be best served by joining an existing local partnership or finding one by researching opportunities nationally.

Join a Local Partnership

Trainers or breeding farm owners are usually the people who offer partnerships or manage them. There are exceptions as it is feasible that anyone could put together a partnership offering providing he or she can gather a pool of investors, act as the managing partner, and either hire a trainer or contract with a farm to provide the services necessary for the partnership.

To find trainers or farms offering partnerships in your area, contact the Thoroughbred Owners and Breeders Association (859-276-2291). Although you might call the racing associations in your area, most state breeders' organizations or the local track probably won't have the information you need readily available. TOBA, on the other hand, is in the business of helping people like you, and the staff is friendly and accommodating. Even if they find it impossible to pick the information off a shelf, they will go out of their way to get it for you. You can find out more about TOBA under the Resources section at the back of this book.

The Thoroughbred Owners of California (TOC) provides a similar service. This organization has lists of partnerships within the state, which you will find helpful. Neither TOBA nor TOC will recommend a specific managing partner to you, but they will give you a list of several partnerships to call.

In 2001 TOC published a list of members who offered partnerships in California, including those who offered racing partnerships and those who offered breeding partnerships. That report revealed the following figures:

• Typical investment: from as little as $1,000 to $3,000 to as much as $150,000, and a median of approximately $10,000 to $25,000.

• Average monthly charge per horse: most respondents anticipated $2,000 to $3,000.

• Percentage of purse charged: Many said "none." Those that did, stated a number ranging from 2 percent to 12 percent, with the most common being 5 percent to 10 percent.

• Average size of partnership: from two to twenty, with most partnerships comprising five to ten people.

Although both TOC and TOBA will provide phone numbers of trainers or breeding farms, the racing secretary's office at each track also keeps track of the barn assignment and phone number of every trainer stabled there. If you know the track where the trainer you want is stabled, the racing office personnel there will probably give you his or her number if you tell them what you are calling about. If they won't, ask them to have the trainer call you. Obviously, if you are just getting started and want to enter this sport without investing a lot of money at the get-go, you shouldn't bother the already-famous and most successful trainers. There are many good trainers at every track who are building their business and who will be eager to work with you.

Or rather than calling the racing secretary's office, stop by and introduce yourself. Anyone working at the track should be able to direct you to the office. It's worth popping your head in the door, even just to look around. Depending on the time of day, you may find a great deal of hustle and bustle; this is not a calm corporate office with executives tucked away in quiet corners. Dozens of people may be milling about, deep in conversation. You'll find yourself looking for a concierge, but you won't find one. Just step up to the counter and tell someone what you are looking for and that you would like to contact and interview two or three trainers who offer the type of partnership you are interested in. Be forewarned, however, you may not get a straightforward answer, as a good system of bringing together managing and prospective partners doesn't yet exist at the local racetrack level.

The Internet may have some of the information you need, but in order to find it you may have to spend a lot of time sifting through sites and hitting dead ends. Therefore, the best route is the direct one. Well, the almost direct one. That is, talk to the people who work with the people you want to meet. That's the reason to go through TOBA or TOC. They can get those names and numbers a lot easier than you can. (To the best of the author's knowledge, California is the only state that has an organization like TOC to work with. TOBA is a national organization and can best serve Thoroughbred owners in all the other states.)

If you aren't sure which type of partnership you want to get into, ask the people at TOBA or TOC for a referral to two or three trainers who have racing or claiming partnerships available, and two or three breeders in your area who offer breeding partnerships. They may also know about pinhooking opportunities, which aren't as common. If you are interested in pinhooking, ask the farm owners and trainers you meet and interview about it. All of them have a network of people to whom they can refer you.

These efforts will provide you with several names locally. After talking with the trainers or farm owners listed, you will have a better idea of how you want to be involved and what to expect. Just don't be shy. Take that first step.

Research Opportunities Nationally

As we discussed in chapter 2, you may not mind if your horse isn't stabled nearby. In fact, you may prefer the idea of taking a break to visit a distant track or farm. If, in your search for the most suitable partnership, you decide to cast a wider net, you can certainly be more selective. Hundreds of opportunities await you. You may choose a location where you like to vacation or a city in which you know you'll find more experienced managing partners.

Early in 1999, I sent a query letter to all horsemen offering partnerships that were listed in *The Source*, a directory published by *The Blood-Horse* magazine. Of the 220 people offering partnerships in that publication, sixty-eight responded by letter, a phone call, or both.

The most expensive partnerships offered comprised only two or three people investing $50,000 or more apiece for a single horse. At the other end of the spectrum were partnerships that allowed people to buy in for only a couple hundred dollars with no maintenance fee. These partners own a miniscule part of one horse and are probably not going to do much more

47

than follow that horse's career. Furthermore, financial success is unlikely.

Summing it up, if you are open to a partnership in any part of the country, you'll hit many of the same sources you would to find a local partnership, only you'll throw your net much wider and get a lot more names.

Interviewing Managing Partners

The managing partner, as used in this book, may be called by a variety of titles in the legally binding partnership agreement. In all cases, however, that person is responsible for overseeing the partnership.

The managing partner must deal with a myriad of issues: business and tax laws, protecting the enterprise with adequate insurance and operating procedures, hiring and overseeing staff, directing the horse's career, and so on. When a horse farm owner or trainer offers partnership opportunities to the public, don't assume all of these details have been properly addressed. While showing respect is appropriate when you interview candidates, it is also important you are satisfied that this person not only is licensed but also conducts business professionally.

Once you buy into a partnership, every person in your group must understand that although he or she may make suggestions, the partnership operates not by vote but by the managing partner's directive. The managing partner may solicit input but is under no obligation to follow the advice of the partners, even if they are unanimously against him. Your agreement may allow for you to fire him, but as long as he is the managing partner, he will have authority to make decisions.

When you join an existing partnership, making sure you are comfortable with the managing partner is every bit as important as the financial "good deal" you may uncover. If you are considering offerings around the nation, you will probably do most of your initial interviewing over the phone and eventually meet just a few candidates face-to-face. What are some of the things you should ask?

The Telephone Interview

Experience: How long has this person managed partnerships? You may not need someone with twenty years of experience, but you also don't want someone who is managing his or her first partnership. You'll want to know whether any of his partnerships have been profitable and how long his partners have been with them.

Written Agreement: Every partnership should be controlled by a written contract or agreement, no ifs, ands, or buts. This topic is covered in detail in chapter 7. After all, you may have chosen a partnership to protect yourself from liability. The agreement should make clear who is in charge and how much voice each partner has.

Objectives: Are the objectives clearly stated in the agreement? You may want to ask if this manager offers partnerships with different objectives and for examples of success stories.

Referrals: It is very important to ask the managing partner for the names of two or three people who are currently partners. Call these people and inquire about the good and bad experiences they have had with owning a Thoroughbred and with this manager in particular. You'll want to know how long they have worked with him and what their experience in the industry has been. Be sure to ask open-ended questions. "Tell me about this," "What would your advice be to someone in this situation," or "Can you explain to me about…?"

Other issues: Ask how many people will comprise the partnership. If there are too many, your managing partner is likely to become overwhelmed with administrative duties.

Find out what percentage of the partnership the managing partner will own. He is in business to make a profit and must do so whether or not the partnership does. That's why trainers and breeders charge a day rate. All of their expenses, as well as personal income, are included in that day rate so they can stay in business whether their horses win or lose money. If, however, the manager owns a piece of the partnership, he has additional incentive to make it succeed.

Ask whether he will be putting in actual cash or just services for his share. Sometimes, as is often true in the case of a farm that manages stallions, the managing partner receives one or more shares for his work and the liability incurred.

If the written agreement clearly states that making a profit is important, then the managing partner can decide to cut costs early, before profits are eaten up. That will not guarantee a profit, but it may help with a decision to sell a horse or enter it into a claiming race before it ravages the bottom line.

Following that thought, make sure you aren't part of the problem. Managing partners sometimes complain that owners fall in love with a given horse and won't let go when it's time. That's understandable. If a horse has shown promise and won a race or two, it's tough to know how patient to be when it goes through a series of injuries or losses. Having a clearly stated profit objective can help in deciding whether to keep a horse.

The Face-to-Face Interview

After boiling it down to two or three candidates, consider visiting each prospect at his or her facility. One of the most important aspects of a rewarding experience with your horses is whether you are having fun. Is this prospective managing partner someone you can enjoy and have fun with? Is he or she someone you can respect?

Be observant. The way people keep their facilities, use their tools, and interact with their staff says a great deal. No one is perfect, and you must understand that this professional works here every day. It isn't a show-place. Although there are lovely farms and trainers who border on fastidi-ous, they represent the exception, not the rule.

Ask to see a copy of the monthly or quarterly report sent out to a typical owner (see "Appendix B" for an example of a monthly billing statement). Reviewing this with the manager or a staff member will ensure that you know how to read it and will help you better anticipate expenses that are to come. Look to see whether expenses are itemized or only a total for the period shown. As an owner, you will have a right to see the books of the partnership. Even though you are not a partner with this person just yet, he or she may be willing to show you how such matters are handled.

While visiting, pay attention to whether the managing partner asks you questions. Remember, this represents a sales call, and you can expect the managing partner to put his or her best foot forward. But you also want a manager who is a bit fussy and only wants partners who are realistic and reasonable.

Interview Topics and Questions

The following is a list of sample questions to ask the managing partner when you visit for an interview. Use this list to get started, but then tailor your questions to your own situation.

• How long have you offered partnerships?

• Do you offer more than one type of partnership?

• How long does a given partnership typically last?

• Of the partnerships you've handled, can you approximate the percentage of them that were profitable?

• How do you feel about using other professionals, such as a bloodstock agent, for advice?

• When making decisions about breeding, what kind of importance do you place on dosage, nicking, and other such matching techniques?

• How often do you use the services of a veterinarian, as opposed to doing as much as possible on your own to keep costs down?

• How much investment would it take to get involved with you?

• How often might you make a capital call or maintenance fee request?

• How often, or when, do you send out earnings or profits to the partners?

• What kind of reports do you prepare, and how often are they sent out to partners? Are there samples to look at?

• Are there current partners with whom I might speak?

• If you can't find a buyer after a horse has finished its course, what do you do with it?

Start Your Own

Although not common, it is possible to form a partnership yourself. You may have friends or family who want to join you in co-owning a Thoroughbred. Maybe one among them has the ability and is willing to accept the responsibility and liability of acting as the managing partner. He will have to work with an attorney in putting together a written agreement that describes the objectives and parameters of your partnership. He will also want to find the people who will help your group in purchasing your horse(s) and in finding a farm or trainer who will oversee the day-to-day care of your horses.

Remember that there are two things that must be managed here. The first is the partnership or business that was created to own the horses and that will be held accountable for handling all assets and liabilities. The second part of the operation is dealing with the animals held by the partnership. Depending on the type of partnership, you will want to have the best farm owner or trainer you can afford whose specialized knowledge will help your business venture succeed. If you start your own partnership, unless one of the partners is a professional horseman, you will have to hire others to manage your horses' careers.

At the beginning of this chapter, we discussed how to find trainers and farms that offer partnerships to the public. In most of these cases, the person presenting the offering will own at least a percentage of the horses in question. He may have bred or purchased a horse with the intention of syndicating it.

(Note: The word "syndicate" in the racing world is most often used to indicate a group of people who own an interest in a breeding stallion. A member of the syndicate would own seasons or shares of the stallion, each season representing one breeding right. The verb "to syndicate" generally means to split into shares and manage as a group and is not bound to stallion ownership. Owning a percentage interest in horses other than stallions is more commonly referred to as "owning in partnership.")

If the managing partner is selling shares of a horse he already owns, find out its original price before you invest. It is possible, of course, for someone to buy a horse and then syndicate it for much more than that original price. This is neither illegal nor unethical, but if the initial price has been doubled, for instance, to ensure a profit just through the syndication of the animal, that makes the horse more expensive than the market indicated. After all, to make a profit you must buy a bargain and keep the costs down. If you pay too much for the purchase of a horse, it makes that profitability much harder to attain.

This is one good reason for starting your own partnership. You can hire whatever professional help you need to find the bargain horse and then hire a trainer or farm owner to manage the animals for your group. You have more control this way and can be assured that you won't be paying more than the market price for horses. It takes more time, of course, to manage your own partnership. You'll have to do a lot of legwork and research on your own and also identify and interview several trainers or farm owners in deciding where to place your horses. But if you make each of these tasks an adventure and include your partners, visiting these people can be very enjoyable and rewarding.

Before deciding to start out on your own partnership, consider and discuss it pretty thoroughly with all those who will be involved. The work and responsibility will be significant for whoever accepts the role of managing partner. Many trainers or farm owners will be happy to work with you if you have your own partnership and managing partner. That means all the responsibility of keeping each member up to date and making final decisions regarding your horse's career will be taken off their shoulders and they can focus on what they do best.

You and your partners may decide that you would like a bloodstock agent to find a horse and represent you in its purchase. He will be paid a commission for doing so, and once you've acquired the animals, he will have them shipped to the trainer or farm manager with whom you have contracted.

If your group wants to give pinhooking a try, one of the members of your partnership can act as the managing partner. He will want to hire a bloodstock agent to represent you in both the buying and selling of your horse and will have to employ the services of a farm to care for and prepare it for auction when the time draws near. Your agent will know of farms near the sales facilities (saving shipping costs) that will provide these services.

When starting a breeding partnership, you may want to see if the farm being used wants to buy in. Just make it clear that you have an assigned managing partner who will make final decisions about the horse.

The farm may already own horses that meet the criteria of your group. If the farm offers to sell one to your group, consult your bloodstock agent. You want an objective opinion before you make your purchase.

Secondly, the farm may accept a percentage interest of your enterprise in exchange for the normal day rate that would be charged to the partnership. This provides a mutual benefit. The partnership can operate without needing as much cash flow, and the farm only covers actual expenses, contributing its service at a wholesale level.

Sometimes finding a prize offering is a matter of remaining flexible. The farm, or agent, may have ideas you haven't thought of. If you always keep it fun and stay open to ideas, you'll enjoy your experience more.

Once you decide on a trainer or farm to oversee your horse, make sure everyone in your group is committed to following his advice. Neither trainers nor farm owners are miracle workers, and you must be willing to give them enough time to work with your new acquisition to see what develops. If your horse doesn't start winning right away, or there is a setback at the farm, don't be too quick in deciding you've chosen the wrong person. Any number of factors could be at play, including the horse itself.

No matter which type of partnership you choose, using the right strategies, selecting the right partners, and diversifying your interests will help you from losing money so quickly that it takes you out of the competition. If you can stay in the game long enough, opportunities will come your way, and those occasional winners may bring in more than enough to offset the cost of those that did not win. Protect the down side, and the up side will take care of itself. The goal is to get involved in an enterprise that will bring you the greatest amount of fun while you try to make a profit.

Evaluating Trainers and Farmers

We've already discussed how you can get a list of breeding farms and trainers by contacting TOBA, TOC, and other organizations. Once you have your lists, how do you narrow it down to just a few people to interview? This is especially onerous if you are conducting a national search. There are thousands of candidates to consider, so where do you start?

First, let's look at trainers. The daily program at your local track will list those trainers that have been most successful at that race meet. Additionally, you can use the Internet to research the performance record of all trainers at any track throughout the country. The *Daily Racing Form* also lists the performance record of each trainer for each race listed.

When you review which of these people to contact for an interview, you will want to ignore the most successful and the least successful. The most successful trainers will already be working with experienced owners who are spending large sums of money for each horse. They also will tend to have bigger operations and will not have much time to spend with someone just learning the business.

Conversely, the trainers at the very bottom of the list are risky. There is no doubt that some of those trainers may simply be new in the business or have not had an opportunity to work with the better horses. Or things just haven't fallen their way yet. As a beginner, however, you don't want to enter this industry with someone who is already struggling. It's better to find a trainer somewhere in the middle of that group, one who has had some success and yet will have enough time to share his or her experience and knowledge with you.

Seek the input of successful trainers who might not be able to take you on. They know the work ethic and personalities of the up-and-coming talent and could give you a good lead. Also, ask the jockeys. Everyone recognizes genuine talent. When these professionals express respect for a given trainer, even if he or she is just getting a foothold on a career, that's a good sign.

When interviewing a trainer, consider asking the following questions:

• How many horses do you have in training at the moment? How many do you consider optimum?

• How many people work for you, and how long have they been part of your staff?

• What is the average value (or purchase price) of the horses in your barn?

• How many owners do you work for? How many are individual owners as opposed to owners in partnerships?

• What circuit do you follow? That is, what tracks do you run your horses on and what is the annual schedule?

• How do you track what is happening in the development of each of the horses in your care? Do you keep written records of this? What reports are sent to the owners? Will you show me samples?

When asking these questions, your point is not to find a right or wrong answer but to open topics of discussion that will help you know this trainer. The more you understand your trainer's preferences and the way he or she works, the more likely it is that you will have a satisfying experience together.

What about selecting the right farm? This list, also, is vast, as there are farms in almost every state. In North America for the year 2002, 4,111 stallions were bred to 63,253 mares, producing approximately 38,523 foals. The states having the largest focus of breeding farms are Kentucky (29.7 percent), Florida (13.1 percent), and California (10.3 percent). Other states with a significant number of Thoroughbred breeding farms are Texas, New York, Louisiana, Maryland, Oklahoma, Washington, Illinois, Ohio, and Pennsylvania.

To enjoy the best experience, you might start by visiting a few of the farms in your locale. After all, a horse farm is pretty much the same everywhere, and each one provides similar services.

Farms, however, also earn reputations. Asking for referrals and seeking the advice of professionals that work with a number of horse farms can be of great value. There are also a number of criteria to consider. You'll want to know how long the farm has been in existence, how long it has been under the current management, the size of the operation and number of staff, and so on. Check out the facilities and pay attention to practical things: How happy does the staff seem to be? How expensive are the horses that are kept on the farm? Have any of those horses distinguished themselves?

After meeting and interviewing these prospective trainers and horse farm owners, you will then need to trust your own judgment or gut feeling. Do you and the others in your group feel you could work with this individual over a long period? If so, it may be a good opportunity for both of you. If you are prepared to accept losses along with wins, you will have added a professional to your team who will do all that is possible to make you a success.

5

Finding and Keeping
the Right Horse

S everal considerations go into choosing the right horse, including price, pedigree, and conformation. A bloodstock agent can provide expertise in helping you with your choice. In addition to understanding bloodlines, bloodstock agents develop an eye for conformation, action, and weakness.

Bloodstock agents earn a living buying and selling stock for clients, and even the most successful owners rely on their expertise. Although it can vary, their normal commission is 5 percent of the purchase or sale price. As experts on conformation and pedigree, bloodstock agents have a solid grasp of market value, which can be invaluable in finding bargains and avoiding bad investments.

In addition to buying and selling stock, bloodstock agents can also advise which sales would be best for you to attend; point out stallion and brood-mare crosses that are likely to produce good foals; and provide a network of colleagues, trainers, farm owners, and others you may want to meet when you are forming a partnership. They can sometimes negotiate the cost of breeding seasons below advertised fees.

Also, most bloodstock agents know many of the consignors at the sales. Consignors try and get the best price they can for their charges and may elect to tell you only the rosiest side of the picture. If they are answering the questions of an experienced bloodstock agent, however, they are much more likely to disclose information. After all, consignors may only see you once in their careers, but they will have to play ball repeatedly with the agent.

If you would like to talk to a bloodstock agent, your managing partner may have already established a relationship. If not, suggest that the two of you meet with one. You may also contact the Thoroughbred Owners and Breeders Association (TOBA), Thoroughbred Owners of California (TOC), or one of the sales companies to ask for referrals. Most state Thoroughbred organizations publish industry directories, and many agents are also listed in *The Source*, published by *The Blood-Horse*.

The bloodstock agent will discuss what you are looking for and how much money you are willing to pay. He will help you at the auction and make plain any gray areas. Remember, the key is to find a bargain. In his autobiography *Dirt Road to the Derby* (Eclipse Press 1999), trainer Bob Baffert explains how he and owner Mike Pegram found their success. "We never had much luck buying expensive horses, so we didn't like spending over $100,000 for a horse. We'd go for numbers and try to pick up little freaks. That's where we had most of our success. For example, I paid $37,000 for High Stakes Player, and he's earned over $800,000."

Finding the "right" horse takes effort. If you needed a new outfit, you wouldn't grab the first one off a rack at the nearest store, nor are you likely to find a prize in a horse without doing a bit of shopping. First, educate yourself about the basic issues of pedigree, conformation, and the like. Next, hire a professional agent to scout out the bargain possibilities. Maybe your baptism into racehorse ownership will be a partnership that has already purchased its horses. But if you do get the opportunity to be involved in the selection, you'll be ready to take on the challenge.

Pedigree

The first thing a prospective owner looks into is a horse's pedigree. Understanding a horse's pedigree involves knowing about its predecessors on both sides of the family and how they did on the racetrack. All of this information is available on the Internet through The Jockey Club's EquineLine or from Bloodstock Research's BRISnet (see Resources section at the end of this book). These sites provide pedigree reports in easy-to-read chart form.

Auction catalogs also provide similar information, but are edited to present the horses being sold in a more favorable light. Your agent, trainer, or managing partner can help interpret this information.

Pedigree reports indicate not only why a horse shows value but also what kind of things you might expect from it. For example, a pedigree can indicate whether a horse might be a sprinter or a long-distance grass runner. Knowing how a horse's paternal and maternal ancestors have done will indicate its potential strengths. The report will also let you know if any older brothers or sisters are doing well. This information can't guarantee your horse will be a winner, but it's as good an indication as you can get.

Pedigree and price usually correlate. A yearling by leading sire Storm Cat out of a stakes-winning and stakes-producing mare can expect to fetch millions at the exclusive summer yearling sales. Proven performance in a pedigree increases a horse's value. Conversely, a yearling by an unproven sire out of a young mare that has yet to produce a winner necessarily would cost less.

Conformation and "Action"

While pedigree is important, a lot can be learned by examining a horse's conformation. Conformation refers to how a horse is built, both in its skeletal frame and muscle mass. In addition to guessing whether the horse will have the build of an athlete, the owner must feel assured that it can withstand the rigors of racing. On the video *Conformation: How to Buy a Winner* (Blood-Horse Publications 1998), Reiley McDonald, whose Eaton Sales is perennially a leading seller of young horses, says, "Conformation is a game of angles and lines. The straighter the angles and the straighter the lines, the less likely a horse is to have soundness problems." In the same way a race car with a bent wheel or misaligned gears would fall apart when going through the stress of racing, so will the weakest points of a horse.

Countless books and videotapes have been produced on conformation. If you haven't been a horseman for long, you may feel you need a dictionary to follow along when experts discuss the conformation of horses. Both TOBA and the TOC periodically sponsor seminars on the subject. *The Horse Buyer's Notebook*, published by Russell Meerdink Company, helpfully illustrates each of the points to look for while evaluating a horse's conformation.

For our introductory purposes, the areas to consider first are balance and symmetry in both bone structure (skeleton) and in mass (muscles). Is this animal beautiful in proportion without looking awkward? Its height, length, and width should correspond to and complement one another. A general rule of thumb is that the body should divide relatively into thirds. And although the head shape isn't critical, does it look like it belongs on this particular body?

After getting a reading on the horse's balance and relative proportion, look for flaws. As McDonald pointed out, it's about angles and lines. Is the spine straight? Do the legs fall straight to the ground without bowing in or out and without being crooked or twisted?

Next, pay attention to the horse's muscular proportion. Like in any other animal, a horse's muscles can be built up through exercise and will be in varying stages of development, depending on age and gender. Nevertheless, the basic build of each horse will be passed down from its parents. This is the benefit that owners seek in selecting the right sire to mate with their mare. The evidence is irrefutable that traits are passed down through pedigree lines, and they show up in conformation. Most importantly, the horse must have strong hindquarters (as those are its engine) and strong shoulders to handle the propulsion. All of these aspects of conformation can be seen while the horse stands still.

You must also observe how well the horse moves. This is referred to as its "action," or "way of going." It's an education to watch experienced people buying horses. They stand in one spot and ask the groom to walk the horse away from them and then directly toward them. Sometimes they do this a couple of times. Or they may also ask the groom to run alongside the horse so the buyer can see how it lifts its feet while it trots. The buyer is looking for a fluid and natural motion. If the animal looks like it is fighting itself or struggling for balance in these basic movements, it could mean that these traits will be exaggerated when it races.

Just watching a horse walk to and from the paddock is fascinating. You can see how a horse that looks perfectly straight in its conformation may swing its legs in and then back out. This is known as "winging." Just the opposite, swinging them out and then in, is called "paddling." Both of these movements cause the horse's action to be less efficient than if its legs move in straight alignment. These irregularities also can cause the horse to stumble over its own feet or rap itself in the ankles. On the other hand, some of the best and fastest runners that have ever hit a track possessed ill-conformed legs, although those horses are more the exception than the rule. Stories abound about horses that had a flaw in conformation or in their way of going and turned out to be very fast indeed.

After studying the movement of horses for a while, you may find yourself watching the "way of going" of the people walking ahead of you on the sidewalk. It's surprising how easy it is to see a lack of smoothness or the misalignment of a joint when you start paying attention. It takes awhile, however, to assess how important a certain flaw may be. These are the things a bloodstock agent, trainer, or breeder will be looking for before he or she decides how much to bid on a given horse.

Sometimes a flaw in conformation is obvious even shortly after a horse is born. Yet you cannot always know whether the youngster will simply grow out of its awkwardness. Looking at a foal is a lot like looking at a human baby: You can tell if all of the parts are there, but you cannot predict how the youngster will develop. There is simply no indication whether it

In assessing physical make up, look at a horse from all angles.

will become an athlete. You must wait until it matures to see whether it has the build and balance to compete.

This is the primary reason the pinhooking segment of the horse industry has grown so rapidly. Weanlings and yearlings are the most common candidates for pinhooking. Horses in these age groups provide an opportunity for the speculator to buy just before a horse's next growth spurt and then resell when it begins to blossom a few months later. The price for the same animal may jump tenfold at each successive auction without the horse's ever having entered a race. This huge jump in price takes place when a buyer can more clearly see both how the horse is conformed and how smoothly it moves.

And unless you are willing to pay astronomical prices for those horses that seem to have no flaws at all, finding the "right horse" for your purposes will also be a matter of assessing the importance, or lack of importance, of any given animal's imperfections.

Weaknesses

As you become more familiar with conformation and action, take the time to understand some of the more serious vulnerabilities common to the equine. You don't have to possess the knowledge of a veterinarian, of course, but if you are aware of a few of the ailments common to horses, you won't be surprised or befuddled if and when such a condition happens to your animal.

Most of what is presented in the following section is for those who may have joined a partnership for the first time and are not familiar with the problems horses encounter. Even if your horse never has such a problem, you will hear these things discussed and should be aware of them.

1) Health Problems and Accidents

Horses, of course, are vulnerable to common health problems just like any other animal. They may catch a cold, come down with a disease or virus, be susceptible to parasites, and so on. Just like people, some animals seem impervious to almost all maladies while others always seem to be sickly or accident prone. If you stay in the game long enough, without a doubt, you will own some of both types.

Certain maladies will plague all horses from time to time and colic provides a good example. We have all heard of colic. Colic is actually abdominal pain that can be caused by a number of things, including eating too much food, eating the wrong food, stress, and disruption from routine. That may not sound like a big problem to someone who has not worked around horses, but many a horse has died a horrible and painful death from it. Just watch how concerned a trainer becomes if his or her horse comes down with colic.

For horses and people, probably nothing is of greater value than good health. However, achieving success also requires getting past the land mines of life.

Early on, parents pray that their youngsters make it through their childhood unscathed. If you are the owner of a young racehorse, your prayers

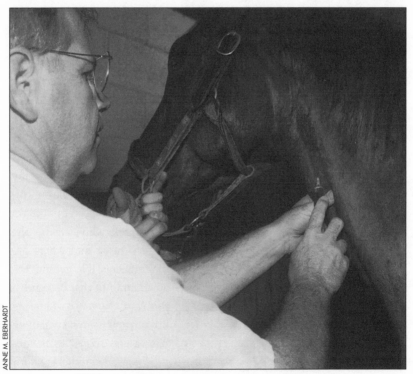

ANNE M. EBERHARDT

All horses require veterinary care from time to time.

will be very similar. For like the young of every species, horses love to frolic, run, play daredevil, and crash into each other. They, too, will scrape their knees, twist their foot in a hole, and knock their heads when they fall down. Then they get up and start darting around all over again. It's almost more than a parent, or a concerned owner, can stand to watch.

Even after the start of its racing career, a young horse can hurt itself in its stall or during training. And when it finally begins to train at speed and to race at its full thousand-pound weight, those comparably thin and fragile legs take quite a beating.

You'll hear about "bone chips," (broken pieces of bone that may have to be surgically removed), "bucked shins" (an inflammation in the front part of the cannon bone), a "quarter crack" (referring to a very painful crack in

Horses can be accident prone.

the horse's hoof), and so on. Some of these problems can be corrected with relative ease, but others may end a racing career.

2) Lungs and Heart

Breathing problems also plague racing Thoroughbreds. Put a human athlete on a track, and it's the lung and heart capacity that will typically limit him or her. While our cardiovascular system breaks down relatively easily, the horse's heart and lungs are magnificent. It's getting the air in and out that becomes a problem. Owners considering buying a new horse will often have a vet "scope" its breathing passage to check for abnormalities. When the lungs call for a tremendous amount of air to be forced through such a small passage during a race, the capillaries in that passage may burst, causing the horse to bleed. The majority of horses that run in the United States are given the drug Salix (formerly known as Lasix) to open the capillaries and retard the bleeding. And while many horses bleed only a minor amount and heal quickly, others (referred to as "bleeders") have a more serious problem.

Dorsal displacement of the soft palate can also restrict a horse's breathing. Trainers try to correct this by using nosebands or tongue-ties whenever the horse is racing and needs a clearer breathing passage.

3) Uncontrolled Enthusiasm

Now enthusiasm doesn't sound like a "weakness" does it? Surprisingly, a third trait that ruins many a horse is its strength and ability to run. Horses are designed to run. Nature made them fast as a natural protection against predators. They know they can run, and they love to run. Put them in open pastures, and they will run for the sheer joy of it.

The problem is, especially when they begin to compete, that they can push their limits too far or run so often as to cause their bodies to break down. When a horse is young its bones are still fragile and can easily fracture, or joint problems can develop from overextension. There is an axiom in horse racing that it's the fast ones that get hurt. It's true. Some horses are born with so much heart and spirit that they push to the breaking point when competing. Many times a jockey will almost stand in the stirrups, pulling on the reins as he tries to hold the horse back and control its pace. And if the horse pushes too much too early in its career it can break down.

One example that comes to mind is a young stallion that only raced three times and is now standing at a farm in Maryland. He won his first start by four lengths. His next race he won by ten lengths. The third race he won by fourteen lengths, but in that race he broke a small bone in his leg. Would it have happened anyway? Maybe. But it's also possible that he could have had a much longer and illustrious racing career if he hadn't displayed quite so much heart: the rest of his body just couldn't keep up. Sometimes an owner will have to exercise judgment and hold a horse like that back for its own good.

There are many things for new owners to learn about horses. Understanding issues not only of pedigree and conformation, but also of the dangers that plague this particular type of animal can help those owners plan better for their horses' healthy and successful racing career.

6

The People in Your Neighborhood

R emember the popular children's television program, "Mr. Rogers"? On each of his shows, Mr. Rogers would sing a ditty about the people in your neighborhood. Then he would interview the doctor, the postman, or whomever the show featured that day so the children would understand what that person does and how his or her job relates to them.

Many of us, not just children, walk right past people without getting to know what they do or how their occupation applies to us. One of the most stimulating benefits of owning a percentage interest in racehorses is unraveling how this sporting industry works. Without a Mr. Rogers to explain the roles the people in these "neighborhoods" play, however, it's easy to take for granted all the work and skill being exercised in our behalf.

What are the responsibilities of those people who handle our horses at either the horse farm or the racetrack? They represent scores of careers, and each of them fulfills a specific need. An awareness of the duties of the major players will give you an appreciation for what is going on and a better understanding of how these people interact.

The Professionals on the Farm

The Horse Farm Owner
A horse breeder has much in common with any other farmer. The factors that affect the success of the breeder's business are basic to agriculture and animal husbandry. If Mother Nature decides to hold back the rain or to let it flow too abundantly, the breeder has problems. A long winter or an exceptionally hot summer can also send things awry. If there's no hay in the fields and feed has to be supplemented with nutritional additives, the ratio of revenue to expense changes dramatically. Every season and every year, farmers live with the anxiety of issues they cannot control.

The person who owns or manages a breeding farm oversees a multi-faceted establishment. A variety of activities happen at the same time and must be coordinated with skill so that the farm makes a profit. Both breeding and foaling (birthing) take place in the spring. If a breeder raises his own crops, or hay fields, they require routine tending. To keep his business growing, the breeder must attend various sales throughout the year.

Most breeders don't own all the horses you see on their property. A breeder may own some of them, and he may also own a percentage of several others. Additionally, many of the horses may be boarders: foals waiting to be weaned or to mature until auction time; broodmares waiting to be bred or to give birth; and, in some cases, horses receiving special care due to injury or sickness (lay-ups).

No matter how many horses are at the farm, however, it goes without saying that the product of a Thoroughbred breeding farm is the offspring. A farm's success depends on the success of the foals born there. How talented these young horses become will largely determine the reputation and future of that farm.

The breeder makes a profit when expenses are surpassed by revenue that comes from stud fees, day rates, the sale of foals, and occasionally other stock. Most horse farms don't stand or house stallions, but some of the large, established farms make their reputations from the stallions they stand.

Stud Fees

Acquiring quality stallions to stand at the farm can take years and sometimes generations. When a champion racehorse worth millions of dollars is retired to stud, the farm owner typically receives four annual breeding rights to that stallion, as well as a monthly fee (the equivalent of a discounted day rate) in exchange for standing and caring for the stallion. It then becomes the farm owner's responsibility to advertise the stallion and oversee the breeding career for the profitability of all the owners represented.

To understand how the breeding rights to a stallion operate, let's use the following example. Farm owner Allen may find a stallion and then talk to his core partners to see if they might form a syndicate to buy the stallion. Conversely, one or more partners may already have been interested in stallion syndication, agreed to commit resources, and authorized the farm owner to look for a worthy stallion prospect. Furthermore, the original syndicate might want to sell additional shares in the stallion.

If the farm owner can find a stallion with both a strong pedigree and a good racing record, getting that stallion booked is not a problem. With the right stallion, getting contracts to cover ninety to a hundred mares in one breeding season is not unusual. But the stallion's reputation alone is no assurance of profitability. The key to success is building the reputation of both the stallions and the farm management.

Over time, broodmare owners come to rely on those who run the breeding farm. They know that quality stallions stand there, and their trust in the people in charge will bring them back. That repeat business is a big factor in making a farm successful. Additionally, as the farm becomes well known, those who own successful horses bound for stud will approach the breeding farm owner to negotiate an agreement to have their stallion stand at that farm. With four annual breeding rights to each such stallion, here is where the farm owner will get his biggest profits.

Day Rates

In addition to stud fees, the horse farm owner receives income for boarding broodmares, foals, and other horses. Owners in a partnership pay a day rate to the farm for the daily care of each of their horses on the farm.

Depending on location, the typical day rate at a farm is between $25 and $35. This amounts to $750-$1,050 per month plus vet, farrier, and incidental bills. These costs are shared on a prorated basis among the owners of each horse. After the mare has given birth to a foal, the day rate normally does not change until the foal is weaned and separated from its mother. At that point, the owner must pay a daily fee for both the mother and the weanling for as long as that young animal stays on the farm.

Sale of Stock

The third major way a farm owner makes a profit is by selling his stock. Because the identity and reputation of a stallion and farm become interlocked, successful stallions usually stand at a farm for the remainder of their life. Broodmares and their offspring, however, are often sold either privately or at auction.

An owner, partner, or competing farm owner may know of a broodmare that he would like to add to his stock. Maybe he feels that mating that particular mare with a stallion standing at his farm will strengthen his program. He would then approach the owner privately and try to arrange a private purchase of that mare. Over time, the farm owner will have an interest in many broodmares, and each partner owning a percentage interest in a broodmare will also own the same percentage interest in her foals. If, for example, you own a 25 percent interest in a broodmare that successfully delivers a new foal every year, you will also own 25 percent interest in a new potential racer every year. Along with the other partners, you will have to decide whether to keep the foal, sell it, or race it. Every partnership has its own objectives that may suggest the right course to take. The farm owner often owns a percentage of the broodmare as well and will enjoy his share of the revenue from the foal.

These are the primary revenue producers for the farm owner. If he owns a percentage interest in any horse that wins purses at a race, sells, or qualifies for bonuses, he will also share in the prorated value of those earnings.

The Farm Staff

The number of people who work at a farm depends on its size. At a small farm, a husband-and-wife team may run the farm with only a few employees helping to handle, feed, and care for the horses. On a large farm, in addition to an office staff, there may be a general manager as well as managers for the stallions, broodmares, weanlings, yearlings, and maybe even one for two-year-olds in training. Each manager would supervise a group of employees in his or her respective areas.

In addition to farm employees, every farm owner has a relationship with professionals such as veterinarians, bloodstock agents, trainers, consignors for sale, and training center managers. If you want additional advice on selecting a good horse for a particular purpose, a farm owner can often refer you to a bloodstock agent that he knows well. If you want to visit the track and your horses, the farm owner can set up an appointment with a trainer for you. This is a tangible benefit of belonging to a partnership. You step immediately into a ready-made package with all of the components in place. You will be treated with the same respect and courtesy as someone who owns 100 percent of a horse. That's a pretty good deal.

The professionals who work on horse farms are specialists, many of them holding university degrees in animal husbandry. The stallion, broodmare, and yearling/weanling managers, and even those who supervise the pastures, fields of hay and grain, and barn facilities have spent years learning to do their jobs efficiently and well. To coordinate all these activities, the farm owner must possess considerable ability.

The Professionals at the Track

The backside of the racetrack, where the horses are stabled and trained, is notably different than a farm. Although the work at both places is focused on the similar goals of caring for and training the horses, the culture is different. At the track there are many trainers, each operating as an individual businessperson and each having his or her own support staff.

This racetrack community contains a variety of businesses that support and serve one another. Veterinarians, farriers, exercise riders, and jockeys go from barn to barn providing services for each business as needed. A track kitchen provides a central meeting place. Vendors bringing hay, straw, food, and supplements arrive each day to provide the supplies the community requires. It is the trainers, however, the people operating each of these small businesses, who make the decisions. They pay the bills and keep the community flourishing.

The Trainer

To be certified and licensed, every trainer must pass a test in the state(s) in which he or she trains horses. This certification tests the trainer's general knowledge of horses. In particular, he or she must demonstrate knowledge of basic equine maladies and medications and how they work. Though trainers are limited as to which drugs they are allowed to administer to a horse, they must have a good working knowledge of numerous drugs and the effect of each on the animal.

Trainers are responsible — and will be held accountable — for everything that happens in their barn or shed row. A detailed log must be kept for all horses regarding exercise and training, health care, drugs that have been administered, and individual problems that may crop up from day to day. A trainer will get to know each horse very thoroughly and oversee its care to make sure that it is kept clean and healthy and develops as rapidly, yet as safely, as possible.

Trainers must register each horse under their purview with the racing secretary of each track where the horse runs. Once the horses are in shape and ready to run, trainers watch the condition book, published by the track every ten days or so, for races to enter their charges in. The racing secretary puts together races based on the number of horses present at the track that fit given categories. Categories include age and gender, number of races won, and types of races. Just because your trainer finds a race for which your horse qualifies doesn't mean the horse will be entered. It takes a sharp mind to discern when to enter a horse and when to keep it out of a given race. Discuss the options and trust your trainer's instincts for choosing a race your horse can handle.

Trainers must be good with horses and people, too.

Although not always the case, the racing secretary will normally not allow barn space for horses that are not prepared to compete. Leeway is given when space is available, but the racetrack is a place where contenders come to compete. When horses are registered at a racetrack, they are expected to be race-ready or to be in training to race. Horses that need rest or additional training can be sent to farms or training centers designed for that purpose. Doing so not only helps to keep the costs as affordable as possible, but also keeps those at the track focused on getting their horses into the competition.

A trainer's job is very much like that of an athletic coach. The difference is that the horse can't talk. Therefore, if the horse doesn't feel well, has an injury, or something else is bothering it, the trainer must be astute enough to ferret out the problem. Most trainers become very good at this. They must also be able to gauge what type and how much of a particular exercise to put the horse through. Horses' temperaments differ, so the trainer must be able to coax the individual to the next level of performance. Sometimes it means pushing them and sometimes just giving them space.

All horses will not be winners, of course. When that happens, which is frequently, a course of action that is "right" may not be clear, and a judgment call is necessary. At times, the trainer working for the owners will have to recommend selling a horse or putting it in a claiming race to move it on. It may even mean taking a loss: cutting that losing streak before it does too much damage. When the time comes for that kind of decision, the owners must have strong faith in the trainer's opinion. To build each owner's confidence then, the trainer must spend time and energy to anchor the partner's trust.

To be successful, trainers must be good not only with horses but also with people. Although much of their day will be spent with the horses in their care, they must handle all the public relations and marketing aspects of the job. If owners become disenchanted, they may move their horses to another trainer or simply quit the business. To keep those owners happy and involved, the trainer must spend time with them and in their behalf. This takes many hours: countless phone calls, updates on the progress of each horse, detailed invoices of expenditures and revenue, hosting social times at the track or over dinner, and whatever else it takes to keep communication open. It is imperative for the trainer to have the owners' confidence. This is especially true for trainers who manage a partnership, as there will come a time when hard decisions must be made, and they will need the support of the entire group.

An astute trainer desires not only a large operation but also good horses. Most trainers feel they can easily oversee the training of twenty or thirty horses. Managing the career of sixty is common, and some of the most famous trainers oversee many more than that at several locations. To become successful, a trainer must have the chance to work with outstanding animals that have the potential to win. The 10 percent bonus that comes from winning purses, especially stakes races, is where the potential profit is for the trainer. The income from day rates just pays the bills. Furthermore, the more her horses win, the more other owners will want to put their quality horses in her stable, which escalates the potential.

The real test of a trainer comes when she succeeds in moving her charges up in class. Even at the lower end of the investment spectrum, it only takes a breakthrough of one or two levels to make money. For example, if an owner brings the trainer a horse that was purchased for $10,000 and she can get him to perform well enough to win a race with a $40,000 purse or place in an $80,000 race she has really accomplished something. And just once in a blue moon, to discover among the many horses in her stable that superior athlete that has physical capacity and heart to gut it out on the track is what makes this career so rewarding.

Grooms and Hotwalkers

No matter how small a trainer's operation, she will always have people who work for her. These backside employees are a dedicated bunch who often begin work at four-thirty or five o'clock in the morning and put in many hours.

Among the variety of people who work for and assist the trainer are the grooms, who feed and water the horses, clean their stalls, and ready them for their daily exercise. Each groom will be assigned certain horses. He will take care of all their daily needs and will be the closest thing to a friend a horse can have.

Grooms and hotwalkers are important members of a horse's retinue.

Hotwalkers work closely with the grooms. They lead the horses around the shed row, an exercise ring, or on a designated path either to warm up the horse's muscles or to help the horse cool down after a race or hard workout. For some horses, that walk may be the only exercise they get on a given day.

Exercise Riders

If a trainer has a large operation, she may have one or more exercise riders that work only for her. Smaller operations rely on freelance riders. Jockeys also work as exercise riders to earn extra income, as well as to establish relationships with trainers they hope to ride for.

An exercise rider receives $5 to $10 for each horse he rides, and the process usually requires no more than thirty minutes per horse. Many exercise riders are too big or heavy to hope for a career as a jockey but are good horsemen who have a sense of how to work the horse and prepare it for racing.

Jockeys

The professional men and women who ride these expensive, athletic animals belong to a unique group. Many jockeys got into the profession following the career of one of their parents or knowing someone connected to racing. Many jockeys begin as exercise riders and then become apprentice jockeys.

Whenever a new jockey's name appears on the racing program, one or more asterisks (hence the nickname "bug") will appear next to it to indicate his apprentice status. After an apprentice has won forty races during a period not to exceed three years, he becomes a journeyman jockey.

To establish his career, a jockey must win a good percentage of his races. This is what will get the attention of the trainers looking for skilled riders. The more races he wins, the better the next horse he gets to ride will be, which will allow him to win more races. This means the rider who can't get his winning percentage up to respectable numbers is not going to have much of a career no matter how much he loves the sport. There simply isn't much money available for those who ride but can't win.

A jockey is paid a fee for riding in a race, whether or not he wins. If he finishes anywhere from last to second place, he may take home twenty-five to fifty dollars. You can't buy many groceries with that. If he crosses the finish line first, however, he gets 10 percent of the winning purse. The total purse is divided among the first- through fifth-place winners with the winner of the race normally getting 60 percent, and the remainder split among the second- through fifth-place winners. In a race for a $20,000 purse, the winner would get $12,000, and the jockey would go home with 10 percent of that, or $1,200. Now that buys a lot more groceries.

Jockeys do not contract with trainers themselves. They have agents to help them build their careers, and at most tracks an agent cannot simultaneously represent more than two jockeys. Jockeys' agents normally charge 15 percent of the jockey's winnings. To earn this money, they develop a relationship with the many trainers at the track and are constantly looking for opportunities that will put their jockeys on the better horses. They may also contract with trainers who have large operations for a jockey to ride exclusively for that stable. If that trainer has a horse running in a given race, the jockey is committed to ride that trainer's horse. If the trainer does not have a horse in a given race, the jockey is free to ride other mounts.

What's it like to ride a racehorse? The horse must have confidence and trust in its rider. Remember that horses love to run, and the really good ones want desperately to win. A well-trained horse has to trust its jockey's judgment regarding pace, the moment to dart through a small opening in the field, or the instant to make the big move. In other words, it must feel the jockey is on its side, helping it to win.

The jockey is the one who has to understand a particular race as well as the other horses and jockeys competing in it, and he must have the ability to make split-second decisions. He must be able to spot just the right hole to move through, determine when he needs a burst of speed, or to hold

ANNE M. EBERHARDT

Jockeys must have a good winning percentage to be successful.

back when the horse is eager to lunge ahead. Sometimes his judgment is wrong or the horse just doesn't have it to give when the rider says "now." But when it's just right, when it comes together between the jockey and his mount, that horse will respond in an exhilarating and marvelous way. Maybe the jockey wasn't sure whether the horse had it in him, but there he is in the winner's circle having joined in an effort just short of being magic.

7

Protect Against Loss/Liability

M ost people who own Thoroughbreds want to have fun, an occasional win, and not lose their shirts. Thousands of people do these
things every year, and you can be among them. If this is your first venture
into the equine industry, however, the cards are stacked against you if you
aren't cautious. Guard against being so eager to have fun that you neglect
to look things over carefully before taking the plunge.

This chapter is intended to help you examine considerations basic to
your safety and security so even if you aren't successful initially, you
won't be hurt to any substantial degree. The most important consideration is how well the partnership you join is designed to meet your expectations. And the only way to know that is by looking over the written
agreement.

The second safeguard we will cover in this chapter is insurance. There
are many kinds of insurance in any field, and you don't want to be extreme
in either avoiding it or feeling as if you need to be covered for every even-
tuality. Somewhere in the middle you will find a balance.

Written Agreements

Some partnerships have operated for years without an agreement or are
using one that lacks specifics. If you happen across either of these situations, it simply may be best to avoid them. If you decide to join a partnership, however, you must insist on a written agreement with specific terms
and goals or turn down the opportunity. It's not worth the headaches and
angst that can come without a written agreement.

It may be that the agreement offered to you is appallingly inadequate.
This is even worse than none at all because you become the new guy on the
block that now wants to change things. How you handle that situation
depends on how bad the agreement is, what you can live with, and what

the extent of your ownership is. The partnership may agree to amend the agreement. They may also tell you to go fly a kite.

At a minimum, a written agreement should include the following aspects:

1) the stated objective of the partnership and a date or result that will determine its end or dissolution,

2) the amount of your investment and what percentage of the partnership that outlay will buy you,

3) a delineation of future expenses that you will be liable for, and

4) the role the managing partner and all other partners will play.

Some agreements will be more comprehensive than this, but these four parameters will make expectations clear.

Goals may vary considerably depending on the type of partnership. But no matter the design, the agreement cannot simply say the partnership will train horses or turn a profit. What does the partnership envision as a strategy and within what time frames? Certainly things will not go according to plan. They seldom do. But if everyone knows exactly what goals the partnership had at the beginning, they will prove very useful in making adjustments when things do go askew.

In any type of partnership, the governing agreement should clearly state your initial investment and how much of the partnership you will own. Once that is established, whether your horses win or suffer defeat, are bought or sold, make or lose money, you will enjoy or suffer that degree of consequence.

You will be assessed for your share of the ongoing maintenance costs and expenses. As explained earlier, this will include the day-rate, medical and dental bills, and any other charges incurred in behalf of your animal(s). It would be a good idea to talk to the managing partner about other expenses that may not be so obvious. Is the cost of acquiring insurance, licensing fees, and so on a part of the day-rate or will these expenses be passed on to the partners? It's best if the agreement spells this outright, as it eliminates any possible confusion. But when it is not stated in the agreement, ask.

In any business it is paramount to know exactly what you are responsible for, where your liabilities lie, and where they stop. If a disagreement arises, how will it be resolved and by whom? This has to do not only with limiting liability but also with all decision making. Will you have a vote or a voice in matters as issues come up? Look for language in the agreement that addresses that. If you think of areas you either do or do not want to be included in, talk to the managing partner about it before signing the agreement. If you want some unique things included that would not affect the other partners, at least ask the managing partner to put those things in a letter so you both have a written reminder of what was agreed upon.

The agreement need not cover every minuscule possibility, but it should make clear what you can and cannot do and what you will and will not be responsible for. After all, even when you arrange to go fishing with a friend, you want to make sure that he will bring the lunch and you will bring the bait. Get one of those tasks mixed up and either you or the fish will go hungry.

Once you have those four basic points covered in an agreement, you can be assured that the most common problems that plague partnerships will not surface. There are always peculiar incidents that bounce into your arena, but having the basics covered in writing will often provide a blueprint on how to tackle anything that arises.

A written agreement need not be formal. It may be called a contract, an operating statement, or just an agreement. The title doesn't matter as much as the content. Most horse racing partnerships will be structured as either a limited partnership or as a limited liability company (LLC). In the past few years LLCs have by far become the preferred legal arrangement. The advantages of each type of ownership will be covered in the following chapter.

The fact is, however, not enough attention has been given to constructing good basic agreements for horse partnerships.

I once went to the racing secretary's office of a major racetrack and asked for a sample contract for prospective owners. What I was given was entirely too general and did not come close to stating liability limits.

See Appendix C for an example of an agreement. Individuals entering into a partnership would still want to make modifications, but this agreement provides a good starting point for touching on the most important issues. Owners associations in many states also offer sample agreements. Just be sure to read them carefully. The fact that it came from a professional association does not guarantee it will serve the purposes of your group as originally drafted. It is a "sample" to get you started.

One reason managing partners drag their feet when it comes to having an agreement drafted is that it is expensive, but you no more want to venture into this business without one than you would set out into a rain forest without mosquito netting. If the partnership you're interested in doesn't have an adequate agreement, ask the manager if he would be willing to review one. Then it may be just a matter of having it modified. While it might cost several thousand dollars for an attorney to draw up a contract for a specific partnership, it should only cost a couple hundred dollars to have a sample agreement reviewed and modified. And that cost would be prorated among the members.

Some people feel that legal documents are just ways to support greedy lawyers. But think about it. Say a horse you own, even in part, broke loose and knocked over a child, causing permanent physical injury. The victim's lawyer would sue everyone in sight. It wouldn't matter if, at the time, you were a thousand miles away and had nothing to do with the horse. Your name is listed as one of the owners. If, however, your contract is carefully written, it could protect you by limiting your liability. That may not stop the victim from suing you, but it could protect you from extreme loss.

What if you decide you've had enough and want to walk away from a partnership? Could that happen? Of course it could, for any of a number of reasons. And if that time should come and there is no agreement at all, how would you manage it? That possibility — and a myriad of other scenarios — should be thought through and agreed upon before you launch out into the deep waters tied to each other.

There are individuals who are petrified at the thought of signing legal documents. A contract?! "Lions and tigers and bears, oh my!" This fear comes from our not wanting to get trapped into something for which we might be liable. A well-written contract (or agreement), however, accomplishes just the opposite. It protects you from unseen liability.

You don't need to be an attorney to read and comprehend an agreement. In fact, if it's written so far above your head that you feel bewildered, it's probably not well written at all. The best safeguard, even if you understand every sentence, is to have your own attorney review the document before you sign it. The attorney's job is not only to read and understand what is written, but also to consider things that could go wrong that are not covered in the agreement and suggest ways that you, and the others, can spell things out for your mutual protection. A further benefit is that your attorney, knowing your situation, may suggest modifications that will be of greater advantage to you.

Watch for the openness of the managing partner when you want to discuss the agreement. You may have identified a weakness in the agreement that was simply overlooked by the others. If the fault is glaring, how do the others (especially the managing partner) respond? One thing to watch for is how reasonable and open your potential partners are. If they simply want to do things their way and aren't willing to discuss your concerns, you may have discovered all you need to know.

The point is to be neither cavalier nor nit-picky about an agreement. If the person responsible for the partnership wants to dismiss written agreements as being a waste of time and money, that's a problem. If you, on the other hand, insist that every "i" be dotted and every "t" crossed and require a fifty-page legal document adequate to protect a Wall Street firm, then you are being paranoid. The degree of ease and comfort you find in discussing such topics is a good indication of how well the partnership will wear over time.

Insurance

The second most important protection against unexpected or catastrophic loss is insurance. It is far more likely that the managing partner will have insurance in place than a well-written contract. Anyone with experience in this business will understand the frailty of horses and how the unexpected can happen. Your managing partner, having seen the unexpected numerous times, will have taken steps to mitigate these losses.

Still, you need to ask the hard questions. What kind of insurance and what amount of coverage has been purchased for the partnership, not just for the managing partner? Again, don't be satisfied with a wave of the hand and "Yeah, sure, I have all the necessary insurance." To assume you are properly covered without looking at the numbers is risky. Once an incidence has occurred, it's too late to go back and fix things. This could truly be a case of trying to shut the barn door after the horse has gotten loose. Make sure it's done now and done properly.

It is, of course, important not to be excessive about it. Insurance can be costly. If you try to protect everything with the highest limits of coverage, you'll have a tough time making a profit.

One good thing about buying insurance in the Thoroughbred business is that most of it has become quite standard. Most owners are concerned about the same things, and precedents have been documented. Your trainer or local equine insurance agent can outline coverage, along with approximate premium amounts, very quickly.

Here's a quick look at the most common types of insurance for this industry. Until the time you are ready to buy into a partnership, however, you may want to just scan the rest of this chapter. It is important as reference material but can be about as interesting as reading the small print in...um, an insurance contract.

Mortality Insurance

Life insurance for your animal may be the most important. If it dies, you lose your investment entirely. Almost everyone purchases this insurance, as racehorses are costly. Normally, a full mortality policy will pay not only if the horse should die by disease but also if it has to be destroyed as a result of an accident while being transported or if it should be kidnapped. On the other hand, to collect from the insurance company, you may have to qualify by proving you did everything possible to save the horse. The insurance company will also want to be consulted about whether to "put the horse down."

The insurance company also determines the fair-market value of the animal, which can vary considerably during the course of a racehorse's life. This will affect both the amount of the annual premium and the payoff in the event of death. Premiums are usually about 5 percent to 6 percent of the horse's value. Although you will probably not be directly involved in either the purchase or cashing in of the policies, you should know what is involved and how it works.

Fertility Insurance

One of the most lucrative ways to get involved in the Thoroughbred industry is with a successful stallion. What a dream to race a young colt and have the thrill of watching him win one stakes race after another. Then when he has made his mark and established his reputation over his racing career, you can enjoy the additional profit of putting him to stud.

Most stallions command a stud fee of several thousand dollars. When his book is completely filled, he will generate a lot of revenue. If your stallion becomes a champion and can exact fees at that level, the horse becomes a money machine. Now what if your famous champion retires from racing, is put out to stud, and turns out to shoot only blanks, as they say? The loss can be terrific, and in this circumstance you couldn't afford not to insure him against infertility.

This happened with the champion Cigar. Although he didn't seem to kick his career into gear until age five, he tore up the tracks the next two years and won a North American record total of $9,999,815 in purse money.

In 1996, at age six, his owner sold a 75 percent interest in him for $18,750,000 with the understanding he would enter stud at Ashford Stud. Even before he garnered his second Eclipse Award as Horse of the Year, his stud fee was set at $75,000. His book quickly filled with mares whose owners were eager to have them bred to this outstanding titleholder. Even though he proved an interested and energetic stud, he proved sterile.

Who could even imagine the shock and disappointment of such news? For almost two years, expert veterinarians tried unsuccessfully to fix the problem. Cigar was retired to the Hall of Champions at the Kentucky Horse Park in Lexington, where he can be seen today. How happy do you suppose the owners were that they had fertility insurance on this guy? They collected $25 million, and although stunned that their champion would have no heirs, they did not suffer actual monetary loss.

Barrenness Insurance

The flip side for the untried filly or mare is barrenness insurance. If you are purchasing a female to get into the reproduction side of the business, you want to protect your investment until you are sure she is capable of conceiving and delivering a foal.

A second strategy that ensures you end up with a live foal is to pay a higher stud fee with the guarantee of a live foal. If the foal dies before it can stand and nurse from its mother, the stud fee is returned. If you choose to pay the reduced no-guarantee fee, make sure you understand what you are agreeing to. In normal no-guarantee arrangements, the fee will not be returned if your mare remains in foal until September. If she loses the foal after that, you will lose the money it took to get her pregnant and all of the maintenance costs during gestation. With an agreement to produce a live foal, however, you have the assurance you can recoup part of your costs. That's especially important if the stud fee was significant.

Prospective Foal Insurance

Barrenness insurance, as we've just described, adds a safety net when you are preparing to have your mare bred. A different kind of insurance, however, is available if you plan to buy a broodmare already in foal.

Say you've decided to get into a breeding partnership. You and your partners have spotted a mare with a great pedigree and racing history that has been bred to a fabulous stallion. Here she is, being sold as a pregnant mare at the next sale, and you think you might get her for a bargain.

What if you make the winning bid and then she loses the foal? Ouch! But if you were wise enough to purchase prospective foal insurance, you may have recovered some of the loss. If you buy a pregnant mare at a public auction, any live-foal breeding contract that the previous owner may have signed with the stud farm is almost always nullified. So you're stuck if the unborn foal doesn't make it. And it will take another year to try again, assuming she has the good fortune to get pregnant right away.

You may also want this insurance if you have sold a stallion season on a live-foal agreement. If the mare doesn't produce a live foal, you will be required to return the stud fee. So why not hedge your bet just a bit and buy an insurance policy that protects you against the loss of the unborn foal?

Claiming Insurance

Should you decide on a claiming partnership, you'll want to look into claiming insurance. It's not easy to obtain, but if you have other horses insured by a company they may also extend the courtesy of this insurance.

As explained in chapter 3, claiming partnerships are fast and fun.

Once you have paid the claiming price, that horse is yours (provided you were the only one to claim him) as soon as the starting gate swings open. Although you don't get the purse if your new acquisition wins that race, the horse is yours even if it breaks a leg or drops dead before the finish line.

If you do not already have a relationship with an equine insurance company, you may have to search a bit and pay a little more. The good news, however, is that if you are able to get your broker to obtain claiming insurance, it is quite reasonable. You will usually pay less than 1 percent of the claiming price. That can buy a fair amount of peace of mind.

Fall-of-the-Hammer Insurance

In a public sale, or auction, the highest bidder becomes the new owner the moment the auctioneer drops the hammer and declares the horse sold. From that moment, the previous owner is exempt from liability.

For this reason those buying at auction may want to purchase an automatic fall-of-the-hammer type insurance. It is usually inexpensive and can be purchased prior to attending the sale. It guarantees that your investment remains secure until your horse is safe and sound in your own barn.

Liability Insurance

Earlier in the chapter we discovered the importance of having a carefully written contract to protect against liability. That's the best first step you can take. The second-best step is to buy liability insurance. This can be purchased on behalf of the partnership and will protect all who are percentage owners. Each owner may also purchase this insurance individually, which may be particularly important if he or she has substantial assets to protect. Someone who has been injured by your horse may go to extreme lengths in a lawsuit if he smells money.

This insurance is a lot like liability insurance on your car. You may purchase coverage at different amounts for property damage as well as personal injury. How much coverage you need will depend on your individual state of affairs. Generally speaking, current rates run about $600 to $800 per year depending on how many horses are in the partnership.

Specified Perils Insurance (FTL)

Specified perils insurance covers only incidents that would take place in an unusual situation. Consequently, it is also quite reasonable to purchase.

Specified perils insurance, sometimes referred to as FTL insurance, refers to death in the event of fire, transportation, or being struck by lightning. It will not pay in the event of death by normal (non-transportation related) injury, sickness, or disease. The cost is about 1 percent of the insured value.

Workers' Compensation Insurance

The law regarding who is liable for injury to employees varies from state to state. In some states, the owner is held liable along with the trainer for whom the employee works. Again, where does your liability end? You need to discuss this with your managing partner and pay attention to what it says in your contractual agreement.

Most trainers are required to carry workers' compensation. If their policy lapses, the track paymaster will withhold purse winnings. Additionally, if a particular trainer's employees have filed a lot of claims, his or her rates will increase. It's good to ask about this, as the increased expense from these fees will be passed on to you and your partners via the day rates you pay.

Wow, buying all that insurance could discourage anyone from getting started. Well, first of all you'll never need all of the available types of coverage. Secondly, remember the basic principle in buying any insurance is to purchase coverage only for what you cannot afford to lose.

A primary reason to buy a racehorse within a partnership is to limit the initial cost. If you can't afford to lose that amount, you might be in over your head. Keep looking. There are very reasonable opportunities available that will provide about as much fun as the more expensive horses.

Nevertheless, as time goes by, your stock may become valuable enough to warrant reassessment of your insurance. In addition to discussing this with your managing partner at the outset, put it in your tickler file every year or two to rethink. A properly written agreement and adequate insurance will help guarantee that you are managing your horse investment as a business. It takes money and effort to succeed in this business, and you don't want to risk a major loss that could wipe you out.

8

Business Structure, Strategies, and Taxes

E ven if you are getting into horse ownership just because you like the excitement of the track, you should have a business plan and structure in place. Unless you operate your endeavor clearly as a business, the IRS will consider it a hobby and disallow deductions, which can help offset losses.

It's a fact that most people who enter this sport lose money, but so do the majority of those who start any new business. The Small Business Association reports that more than 50 percent of business ventures fail within the first year. The reason, however, is not that the ideas were bad, but rather that too many would-be entrepreneurs failed to run their business like a business. An experienced businessperson might have turned a profit on many of those same ventures.

Owning horses is expensive, and you must be ready to make hard business decisions or you can go broke quickly. It's important to sear this next point onto your brain: Don't let your feelings influence your judgment. This includes your dealings not only with people but also with the horses. It is extremely easy to become attached to these animals, especially in your first couple of years as an owner. These horses are gorgeous, big, athletic, and possess huge eyes that are cuter than a puppy's. As you stroke that ultra-soft nose and observe the nobility in your horse's carriage, you fall in love.

You will get to know each one's history. You'll traverse its path of growth and development, sickness and injury, training and competition. You've been down the road together. And when it's time to make some hard decisions to sell, replace, or put these animals down, it can be heartbreaking.

When these times come, and they surely will, you'll have to remind yourself to set aside your feelings. These animals are not pets; they are inventory. Hearing someone say that can sound as hard as granite. But you must remember that only a small percentage of those horses you come to know will be winners. If you are to remain active in this sport, you must be willing to let each one go when the facts indicate it is time. Even if nothing goes wrong, sooner or later your horses will no longer have the capacity to compete or reproduce. As a business owner, you must learn to love and enjoy each animal as long as it is in your care, but be ready to let it go.

You also may have to put a check on your emotions when it's time to say goodbye to members of your team. This may pertain to your partners, the managing partner, trainer, and maybe others. You will have traversed a path with them, too. Having laughed together, worked through problems, been to the winner's circle, and spent time together socially will make calling it quits very difficult. There are times, however, when ending a relationship is the right thing to do, even when you have enjoyed the experience. You may not have to, but be prepared to make those hard decisions if and when you find things just aren't working.

Business Structure

When you first get involved in a partnership, the person who set it up is likely to have decided what kind of legal entity would best serve the group.

How you hold that partnership interest, however, is up to you and can be structured to serve you best. Each of us has a different financial and tax situation. Determining how to hold your business interest and apply the various available strategies to reduce your tax burden and lessen personal liabilities is vital to the bottom line. You will need to discuss your situation with your legal and tax professionals.

In this and the following section, examples illustrate scenarios with which someone reading this book might identify. These are not put forth as recommendations; the author is not a tax or legal professional. If these examples can be used to spark good, thoughtful conversations between you and your advisers, however, they may perform a valuable service.

All partnerships, corporations, limited liability companies, and so on have someone responsible for making the decisions that affect the entire group. Although each legal entity may use a different term for this person, this book uses "managing partner."

No matter what type of structure you choose, there are rules to follow, reports to file, and a number of legal and accounting formalities to "obey" in order to qualify for tax benefits. Are those benefits worth the extra effort? To the right people, you bet! They can be like money in the bank. Once you decide your intent is to make a profit, it becomes a matter of finding the most effective and efficient way of doing so. If you adopt a structure that is more complex than is necessary, it will feel costly and cumbersome. Your goal is to find the structure that is as lean and focused as possible. All costs of breeding, raising, training, and racing a horse are deductible as business expenses if you can prove you have a business plan and strategy that will result in a profit, not just your personal entertainment. With that in mind, let's set out to find that strategy.

Business Strategies

The most common ways of doing business are through a (1) sole proprietorship, (2) partnership (general or limited), (3) corporation (a C corporation, or a regular corporation, and an S corporation, or subchapter S corporation), and (4) Limited Liability Company. If you've not owned a business before, these legal terms may sound intimidating. Those feelings will go away, however, when you get a grasp basic enough to suggest which may work for your business.

Let's use a few simple illustrations. Assuming you are John Doe, you could own your business as John Doe Enterprises. The IRS will then pass all the profit, loss, and tax implications straight through to you as an individual. That is what it means to own a business as a sole proprietor.

If you share the ownership with one or more people, the business entity you and the others create will be a partnership. You will assign a name to your partnership, and everything done within that entity will now be done in its name. The IRS considers your new partnership an "individual." That individual becomes a legal entity authorized to do business in the name you have specified. It may be the "You and Me Partnership" and will be given a special tax identification number so the IRS (and everyone else) will know exactly who is behind the business. Now all the profits, losses, and tax implications will apply to the partnership entity and pass through proportionately to the individual partners.

The third way, establishing a corporation, is just another way to create a new "individual," or entity, with an authorized tax identification number. Usually, a corporation has a number of people who own it; each member's percentage of ownership reflected by the number of shares he or she owns divided by the total shares outstanding.

If the corporation issued one hundred shares and you own ten, you own 10 percent of the company. Normally, more than one hundred shares are issued. Nevertheless, whatever number you own divided by the total shares outstanding will reveal the total percent of the company that you own.

There are two basic types of corporations, regular and subchapter S. Each has particular benefits and limitations. It is rare for individuals to get involved in the business of horse ownership through corporations. If you should run across that situation, discuss it with your attorney and accountant because it will affect you differently than the ways illustrated here.

The Limited Liability Company (LLC), on the other hand, is currently the most popular way of holding a partnership interest in horses. The name may sound heavy, but the structure is not complicated. It's somewhat of a partnership and corporation hybrid. Each state sets its own rules regarding LLCs and basically allows greater freedom in passing through allocated profits and losses while still limiting each member's liability. In the Thoroughbred industry, the LLC has largely replaced limited partnerships.

The following breakdown provides a bit more explanation of each type along with reasons a person would choose one over another. If you envision yourself more in one category, discuss it with your attorney. She or he may help you structure your business along similar lines, suggest options not listed here, or point out disadvantages you hadn't considered.

Sole Proprietorship

This is the simplest way to own a business. The owner does business under the authority of her or his own social security number. She or he would be required to file a fictitious business name statement and obtain a local business license. Using this informal arrangement, she or he is taxed on all the income from the business and can deduct all losses, even against other sources of income, provided she or he has actively participated in the business. The income and expenses of breeding, raising, and racing horses are usually reported on Schedule F of the annual tax return. In a sole proprietorship the owner assumes full responsibility for all liability of the business.

Example: Elaine Hunt recently retired after owning her own travel agency. Over the years, she developed a passion for horses and set aside $15,000 to invest. Having experience at operating a business, she wants to run this activity like a business also and will keep good records. Because she is retired, she can easily meet the active participation test by devoting at least five hundred hours per year. (A married couple could satisfy this requirement by investing this many hours between them.) In this manner, she enjoys the benefits of deducting the initial losses from the start-up costs of entering this new industry against her other sources of outside income.

Partnership

A partnership exists when two or more people form a business with each person contributing any of the following: money, property, labor, or skill. All partners generally share in the profits and losses of the business. In some situations, profits and losses may be allocated using ratios different from the partner's initial contributions to the partnership.

The partnership files a federal tax return and form K-1 to set forth each partner's share of income, deductions, gains, losses, and credits. The partnership itself is not taxed because it is an information return. Instead, the income and expenses are passed through to each individual partner through the K-1.

There are two types of partnerships: general and limited partnerships. In a general partnership, liability for everything done within that partnership passes through to all of the partners. The limited partnership provides limited liability to those partners who qualify as holding a limited interest. Sound confusing? Stay with the thought just a little longer.

All businesses must have someone who can be held liable for the activities of the business. Usually, those who are operating the business on a day-to-day basis are willing to accept this responsibility. Some people, however, want to own and invest in a business but do not want to be held liable for what those managing the business do. For them, holding a limited partnership interest is more attractive.

To accommodate this, a limited partnership has one or more general partners who are responsible for operating the business and making all the decisions. Their liability is not limited. They can sell limited partnership interests to raise the money they need to conduct and grow their business and still maintain control, while the investment-only partners enjoy protection against liability. For many years, limited partnerships were the mainstay in the horse business.

Example #1: Greg and Dave are long-time friends who are as close as brothers. They have dreamed of someday getting into business together as each has something unique to offer. Greg grew up around the track and learned a lot from his father, who owned and trained horses. His schedule is flexible, and he can devote significant time to starting up their business. Although Dave has much less experience with horses, he brings a lot of business savvy to their venture.

Both men's finances are sound, and they have always talked things through before making decisions. As longtime friends, they trust each other and are not afraid of the liability that each will carry for the partnership. Furthermore, they have no worries about the legal fact that either of them could bind the partnership without the other's consent. They choose to draft a simple general partnership agreement outlining their rights and duties.

Example #2: Joan is recently widowed, has loved horses since she was a little girl, and recently went to the track with a friend who enticed her with the idea of owning her own racehorse. However, she has no experience.

There is no way for her to be involved in the day-to-day management of such an enterprise, but she would love to be a horse owner and learn what the industry is all about. Someday she might like to own several horses. But before she decides to go it on her own, her business instincts tell her that owning a winner comes only through years of experience with lots of trial and error. She also is concerned about protecting her other assets from potential creditors or liability loss.

Joan decides to invest $10,000 in a limited partnership that holds three two-year-olds in training. As a limited partner, she will learn what it takes to be a successful horse owner while protecting herself against the downside of losses through liability.

Corporations

Both types, regular and subchapter S corporations, are legal entities requiring the owners to comply with many corporate formalities. Individuals owning and breeding horses seldom use regular corporations for their business because losses of the corporation cannot be deducted by the shareholders. Conversely, subchapter S corporations provide that losses can be passed through and deducted by the shareholders. The income and losses must be prorated on their percentage of ownership, however.

An additional consideration is that shareholders in a subchapter S corporation are generally limited to "resident individuals" only, which in layman's terms means "people." As such, a shareholder cannot be a corporation of either a regular or subchapter S type. In other words, if the partnership is put together as a subchapter S corporation, the prospective owner cannot buy shares in that partnership through his other business holdings if they have been incorporated. When adding this limitation to the fact that a subchapter S corporation is inflexible in allocating profits and losses, you can see why Limited Liability Companies are used much more frequently.

Limited Liability Company

In general a Limited Liability Company (LLC) combines the limited liability of a corporation with the flexible tax advantage of a partnership. This is a newer and increasingly popular type of entity for doing business.

Under the LLC the investor can have much greater control and input, whereas under a limited partnership, investors cannot participate in the day-to-day affairs of the entity. Note further that most LLCs and most limited partnerships are securities and must be registered with the secretary of state where they are doing business.

Example: Let's assume the same facts for Joan that we considered in the example for limited partnerships above. Now, however, let's say that Joan wants to have a voice in the day-to-day affairs of the entity. In that case the

LLC offers Joan the option and flexibility of taking a more active role without exposing her to higher risk.

Business Taxes

If you are mulling over buying an interest in a Thoroughbred, also consider the tax benefits. Although not as generous as they once were, attractive tax breaks are available if you treat your enterprise in a businesslike way.

Many people have heard stories of how years ago it was possible for those in high income-tax brackets to invest in racehorses and deduct huge amounts of expenses and losses against their other income, saving them many thousands of dollars. The tax revisions of 1986 addressed that excess, however, and removed many of those benefits. Consequently, you may occasionally hear someone who has been in horse racing for a long time say something like, "Our industry is in trouble because the Tax Reform Act of 1986 drove away all the owners and ruined the sport." That's nonsense.

Most owners left because they did not work at being smart and also because the purses were not large enough to justify continued participation. It is common sense that if someone goes into business for the sole purpose of generating losses to lessen their tax liability, they aren't in "business" at all! The definition of a business is engaging in an enterprise with the intent of making a profit. Those who were using horse racing only as a way to avoid taxation were missing the point. And in this author's opinion, that Tax Reform Act actually strengthened the industry.

Purses have gone up significantly, and owners have become smarter by treating their horse racing interests as a business. Yes, there are people who want to be in the game simply for the joy of it. They want to own their horses, play around at the track or backside, and treat the entire experience as a lark. If, however, you don't plan to simply throw some money at the sport and do intend to treat your effort as a business, it's to your advantage to squeak out every tax advantage possible. That's what every businessperson does in every industry, and the IRS and government encourage that behavior because it stimulates the economy.

Someone once pointed out that the average American spends more money on taxes over a lifetime than for any other single thing. More than for food, housing, clothing, etc. For this reason, obtaining every available deduction and avoiding unnecessary tax are imperative to all of us. The government provides generous tax advantages to those willing to take the risk of running a business.

Author's note: The rest of this chapter will explain tax law and strategies to gain financial advantage. Those who have sizeable assets or income will be interested in what things are important to the IRS about racehorse ownership and techniques others have used to reduce their tax burden greatly. If you are not in this category, you may want to skip the rest of this chapter.

Seven-Year Loss Provision

The IRS says that in order to deduct losses, an investor's efforts must be "engaged in for profit." To prove that point, the seven-year-loss safe-harbor provision comes into play.

Example #1, A Profitable Scenario: Here's the rule: if the owner shows two profitable years within a seven-year period, the activity will be presumed to be a business starting with the second profitable year. Note that the IRS can rebut the presumption, but the presumption is important and is almost never successfully challenged. The following chart sets forth a ten-year period in which the owner had only two years of profitability.

1990	1991	1992	1993	1994	1995	1996	1997	1998	1999
L	P	L	L	L	L	P	L	L	L

The two years of profit within seven years is more complicated than it may appear at first blush. Generally, the seven-year period in the above example starts with the first profitable year in 1991 and is presumed to be a business in 1996 and the years thereafter. Obviously, it would be best to have two profitable years back to back and early on to establish the presumption. Also an investor or managing partner needs to give some thought to the timing of income and expenses to establish profitable years. For example, to establish a profitable year, an owner might consider prepayment for services or materials, deferring expenses, or timing when to sell horses. Furthermore, a horse may be sold using deferred payment or installments. Such planning can be vital in helping to establish profitable years.

Other strategies should be considered. An investor may want to consider putting smaller amounts of money into several partnerships. Even though a smaller percentage is owned in each, it may prove preferable to investing in only one horse as it demonstrates more business activity.

Example #2, An Unprofitable Scenario: When an owner cannot meet the two-out-of-seven-year safe-harbor standard, he may still demonstrate intent to make a profit through facts and circumstances surrounding the activity. In this regard, an IRS regulation sets forth nine factors that must be considered.

1) The manner in which the investor carries on the activity: he must use businesslike procedures and keep good records.

2) The investor's expertise or that of his advisers: he must seek the advice of experienced counsel in the horse business, such as attorneys, accountants, trainers, farm managers, and veterinarians.

3) The time and effort the investor spends in carrying on the activity: he should log time spent or engage competent personnel who also devote considerable time to the horse activity.

4) The investor's expectation that the assets used in the activity may appreciate in value: it helps to own Thoroughbreds that have a documented history of appreciating in value.

5) The investor's success in other similar or dissimilar activities: being profitable in other start-up businesses helps.

6) The investor's history of income or losses with respect to the activity: the business should show that it is able to make money after a normal start-up period.

7) The amount of occasional profits that the investor earns: even one profitable year is helpful.

8) The investor's financial status: It is better not to have substantial income from other sources. Moreover, a commitment of 10 percent or more of annual adjusted gross income to the activity is helpful.

9) Elements of personal pleasure or recreation that the investor may have experienced: it is not a good idea to use the horses personally for recreation.

The first four factors are the most important. It is very helpful to keep a diary, prepare an annual budget, and have a written business plan showing how you intend to make money.

Material or Active Participation

Even if your entity qualifies as a business, you must also answer whether you participated either materially or passively, as defined by the IRS. If you participate materially, that is to say actively, the losses can be deducted against outside sources of income. If not, no deal. If your involvement qualifies as passive, losses can only be used to offset passive income, such as income from real-estate investments.

Sharing ownership with others, in many cases, may define you as a passive investor since all limited partners are automatically considered passive investors. It is important to note, however, that owners of an LLC are not automatically deemed to be passive investors since they can materially participate without affecting their limited-liability status. This is a subject you should discuss with your accountant. If you should join a LLC, you may have more leeway than you would have had in a limited partnership.

It's also important to remember that each partnership is treated as a separate activity. Thus, cumulative passive losses from any one partnership are only deductible when the partnership interest is sold or terminated. For planning purposes, different partnerships can be structured to terminate one or two years after their inception so that investors can take losses at that time. Sometimes this type of planning is difficult if you have many partners in different financial situations. With the right group, however, each agreement can be structured to order.

Here's another strategy. From a tax-planning standpoint, if you will be defined as a passive investor in your horse ownership, consider other investments you might employ to generate passive income. Say you own some rental property. You might think about taking out a bigger mortgage against your current home and use the proceeds to reduce the debt on the rental property. This would increase the net income on that property. You are eligible to refinance and take up to $100,000 of refinance proceeds and have the interest deductible as home mortgage interest expense. The more passive income you generate, the greater the ability to offset passive losses from the horses.

Example: Bob Smith makes good money and owns a home worth $300,000 that is free and clear. Additionally, he owns two rental properties that have a combined worth of $250,000 and an indebtedness of $100,000. Bob decides to take a mortgage out against his home for $100,000 and use it to retire the indebtedness on his rental properties. He knows he can deduct the interest expense against his home from his ordinary income. That's extra money in his pocket each year. With his rental properties now free of debt, the annual income from those properties increases his passive income, which can now be used to offset the passive losses from his horse business.

Basis and Amount at Risk

Generally speaking, the total amount of loss is limited to the total amount at risk. For most investors, this is the amount of cash contributed to the partnership or LLC, including all amounts borrowed to make the investment. Even after establishing a profit motive, and establishing that the investor is an active participant, the owner can take a tax loss only to the extent the loss proceeds do not exceed the amount of his investment.

Depreciation

The deeper we get into the details of taxation, the more exceptions complicate things. You absolutely want an accountant to help you think through your taxation strategy. Attempting to keep track of all the caveats, the howevers, and unlesses can lead to migraines. Consider the following.

Most owners choose to depreciate horses under the modified accelerated cost recovery system. The recovery of cost through depreciation takes place in one of two systems, depending on the age and type of horse. The depreciation for all horses must be spread over either a three- or seven-year period.

Stated as simply as possible, a racehorse two years old or less is depreciated over seven years; a racehorse older than two years is depreciated over three years; a broodmare, if more than twelve years old, is depreciated over three years; and a broodmare under twelve is depreciated over seven years. There are, of course, exceptions. See why you need your accountant?

If a horse is owned with the intent of resale, it is considered inventory and is not eligible for depreciation. It is also possible to treat the cost of a horse as a deductible expense during the tax year in which the horse is placed in service (the service for which it was purchased). The maximum deduction is $25,000 and will often be most useful for the small investor who purchases only one or two horses a year. If more than $200,000 is invested in the total activity or purchase of a horse in any one year, this deduction is not applicable. When the purchase price exceeds the $25,000 amount, the balance can be depreciated using either the three- or seven-year rule. [For an in-depth explanation, see Arnold Kirkpatrick's book *Investing in Thoroughbreds* (Eclipse Press 2001).]

Selling Horses

All costs of breeding, raising, and racing horses are deductible as ordinary business expenses. If you sell your horse, however, a good portion of the sales proceeds may be treated as appreciation and qualify for the lower capital gains treatment providing your horse was held for twelve months and was not held primarily for resale. From a tax-planning standpoint, this is good because deductions are often taken against ordinary income rates, which were as high as 38.6 percent in 2002. Tax laws and rates change every year, but planning opportunities always exist.

Example: Say the horse you own is older than two and was purchased for $20,000. Two years later, you sell it for $25,000. After taking $15,000 of depreciation, using the three-year cost recovery method, this is what it might look like.

Original Cost	$20,000
Less Depreciation Deductions	($15,000)
Adjusted Basis	$5,000
Sales Price	$25,000
Less Adjusted Basis	$5,000
Total Gain	$20,000
Gain Reported as Ordinary Income Due to	
Depreciation Recapture	$15,000
Gain Subject to Capital Gains Treatment	$5,000

In the above example, when property is sold subject to depreciation recapture, the recapture amount is taxed at ordinary income tax rates and not at the capital gains rate. Moreover, if you used the installment method to defer the gain until payments are actually received, the amount subject to depreciation recapture is fully taxable in the year of sale, regardless of when you receive payments.

Another possibility: Assume the same set of facts with the exception that the horse was sold under the installment method. You receive $5,000 at the time of sale and the balance of $20,000 as a note payable over four years. You would now owe tax at ordinary income tax rates on the full amount of the depreciation ($15,000) in the year of sale even though you only received $5,000 that year. Additionally, you would have to report one-fifth of the $5,000 gain, or $1,000, as a capital gain in the year of sale. So you want to be careful and think ahead. Sometimes, a little forethought can save you money.

Ready for another alternative? When you know you will have a gain on the sale of a horse, it could be deferred by buying "like kind property." You may be familiar with this rule as it also pertains to real estate. When it is used in the case of horses, the replacement horse must be of the same sex and of greater value than that of the horse sold. The basis of the sold horse becomes the basis of the replacement horse and the gain is now deferred until the replacement horse is sold. Clear? Well, if not, give it time and remember trying to plan these things without the help of a professional would be like trying to land a jet airplane without training.

Let's look at another example.

Example: Assume you own a colt that has an adjusted basis of $15,000. You agree to sell him for $20,000 and then buy another colt for $25,000. Part of the deal is that you receive $5,000 in cash and the rest in installment payments. The $5,000 in cash is taxable and the basis in the new horse becomes $20,000.

These ideas and illustrations are put forth here to stimulate your thoughts. Those who teach creative thinking often encourage us to think "out of the box." It might be worth an hour or so with your advisers to strategize ways to use the tax law for your greatest benefit.

9

A Day at the Track

B elieve it or not, some people become involved in a partnership without ever having attended a race. I did. Possibly, a prospect you invite to become a partner may feel leery about going into business with you because he has never been to a racetrack or placed a bet. If that description applies to someone you'd like to interest in joining you, or even to you personally, read on and discover what you can expect on your first day at the track as a new owner.

Morning at the Backside

If you've never before owned a racehorse, your image of spending a day at the track will change significantly. For many owners, spending the morning on the backside with the horses, trainers, and jockeys is what they love best. Especially on days your horse will be tested during its workout or will actually compete in a race.

You'll want to get to the track by 6:30 or 7 a.m. The horses begin to exercise at dawn with the track closing for workouts by 10 or 10:30 a.m. as preparations begin for the day's races. If you want to have time with your trainer, you'd best be early as he or she will be busy with duties throughout the morning and not available to spend every moment with you.

It's a good idea to wear shoes that you can later clean at home, and also bring a comfortable pair to change into when you leave the backside for the rest of your day at the track. As casual dress is acceptable anywhere at the track except the turf club, dress for comfort if you plan to be there all day.

For your first visit, the trainer will give you directions to the gate leading to the backside and will have listed you as a guest. When you arrive, the guard will ask for a picture ID and will direct you to your trainer's barn. After you have obtained your owner's license and have registered with the track, you will no longer have to go through this procedure, and the guard will simply wave you through.

The backside looks a lot like a small town. Depending on the track you visit, areas may be sectioned off like small city blocks with so many barns or shed rows in each section. Some of the larger stables may actually hang out a shingle to help visitors locate them. Other buildings may be more simply marked with letters.

People will be busy about their particular tasks, and you'll see lots of horses, as well as dogs, cats, ducks, and possibly even a goat or two. Horses are very social creatures and get lonely easily, so a trainer often keeps other animals around to relax them.

As the exercise riders guide their mounts from their shed rows to the track to work out, pedestrians step to the side or politely walk to the edge of the road. Horses are the kings and queens of this special ground and have the right of way.

Everyone will be wearing work clothes, including the trainers and jockeys. No pretty silks or suits and ties on the backside. This is a place where sleeves are rolled up and people do hands-on work.

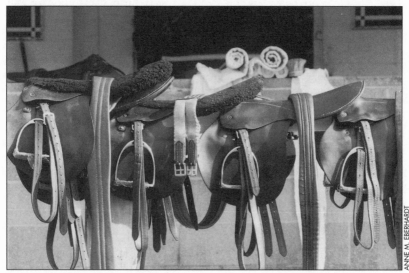

Mornings at the track have unique sights and sounds.

One surprising discovery is how clean and fresh it smells in spite of all the animals and their excretion. The smells are those you'd encounter at a farm. Not the stinky smell of a stale barnyard but the clean smell of stalls with fresh straw and hay. Of course, if you're standing in the right spot at the right time you might get a whiff of a fresh deposit, but overall the back-side is kept very clean.

As you approach your trainer's barn, you'll see grooms saddling horses for their workouts. Horses that have finished their exercise will have their tack (saddle, bridle, etc.) removed and may be led between the barns where the hotwalkers cool them down.

Inside the shed row, you will find some horses undergoing treatment: sore legs, chest colds, injured feet, or whatever. One or more of the animals may be brought out for appointments with the farrier, who will check its hooves and provide new shoes. Later in the morning, when the horses have finished their workouts, they will be given grain, nutritional supplements, and fresh hay.

If you are a novice, use caution in this working area. Lovely as they are, these thousand-pound animals kick and bite. Don't turn your back on them.

A horse's bite is strong enough to turn fleshy areas black and blue and can break small bones in a person's hand. A kick that lands in the wrong place could kill you.

If you feel apprehensive but want to pet a horse, feed it a carrot, or any-thing else, ask the trainer how to do it. He can show you how to approach the horse safely so you won't be bitten, kicked, or stepped on. Also, you should never feed a horse anything without the trainer's knowledge. Stories abound of how simple acts of kindness can turn into nightmares. The authorities suspended a well-known trainer when one of his horses was found to have a trace of morphine in its blood. It took the stunned trainer awhile to learn that someone visiting his barn had fed the horse a poppy-seed bun. Little things can mean a lot. Always ask the trainer before giving the horse a treat.

Your trainer, no doubt, will invite you for a get-acquainted chat in his barn office. This small room may contain nothing more than a desk and a few chairs, a telephone, and a bit of equipment. If you see items you don't recognize, ask about them. You will find an array of tack, or equipment, used on the horses. There will be a variety of bridles and bits, each used for a different situation. Examine them and start to become familiar with this new world. As long as you respect the work and time of those working on the backside, you'll be welcome. Every trainer wants informed owners, and he or she will do what is possible to help you learn.

As you hear, or overhear, new terms jot them in a notebook. Then when your trainer or one of his staff isn't busy, ask for an explanation. You may have to endure a smile at your naïveté, but people delight in sharing their knowledge. If, on the other hand, you're a person who has spent significant time at the track on the front side, you may already be familiar with the lingo and operations of this sport. Even so, it's hard to imagine that spending a few hours on the backside will not be valuable.

This might be a good time to ask your trainer for a condition book. Even an old copy will do for a start. Have him show you how to read it and what the codes or abbreviations mean. Your trainer uses the condition book constantly, and you should understand its importance. In this little book, all the races slated for this meet will be listed. Each race has conditions that entrants must fit. Every trainer at the track is studying this book to determine where to place his or her horses to give them the best opportunity to win.

Will your horse meet the conditions for any of the races listed? You'll find that options are limited and that an experienced trainer will use judgment beyond your current capacity to guide your horse's career. As you discuss the possibilities, you will learn additional aspects of racing strategy.

The more comfortable you become with the condition book, the better you will understand the differences between sprints and routes, claiming races, handicaps, allowances, and classics. Have your trainer talk about his experience with each and when and if your horse might qualify for any of them. Soon the language of racing will become familiar. You'll find the strategy and thinking behind your trainer's decisions come together like pieces of a puzzle.

And please, be careful about expressing an opinion about where and when your horse should compete. You don't want to come across as trying to call the shots just because you've learned a few terms and can read a condition book. As you might expect, it is imperative for the owner and trainer to trust each other. You must allow your trainer to make the decisions you hired him to make. Many owners inadvertently fall into this trap and can end up spoiling an otherwise terrific relationship.

No one will question that the owner is boss. Even as only one member of a partnership, you, too, are an owner. It is your horse, your investment, and, for the most part, your risk at stake. It is the owners who hire and fire trainers. On the other hand, if you take the position of overriding the decision and judgment of your trainer, you are assuming you are more qualified. That can be a huge blunder. Don't join a partnership unless it has a trainer in whom you have confidence.

You can see horses work out on the track every day, but not every horse in your trainer's barn will exercise daily. Even human athletes give their muscles time to rest and rejuvenate. On some days the trainer may be working on muscle development; on others, endurance; and yet others on allowing for recuperation and healing. In younger horses the trainer may focus on teaching discipline, obedience, breaking from the gate, or other situations they will encounter in competition.

After watching the exercise riders or jockeys saddle up and get instructions from the trainer, you'll now have the opportunity to watch the rider and his horse do their thing. As you stand on the observation platform, you will see dozens of horses going around the track in both directions. On North American tracks, horses race counterclockwise. When the exercise riders are just walking their horses or warming them up with a slow trot, they take them on the outside perimeter of the track and in the opposite, or clockwise, direction. In part this signals to the horse that this is just a warm-up or cool-down.

Horses may work out at a gentle trot around the track one or more times, gallop at an easy pace, or be pushed to run for time at a certain distance, which is called breezing. When a breeze is to take place, an official at the racetrack, called the clocker, must be notified. This person will use a stopwatch to time the horse over a certain distance. This public information will be printed in the *Daily Racing Form* and often in the daily program. A horse must have had a public workout (or "work") within thirty days prior to the race. Also, as the track is not a place horses are allowed to just hang out, the racing secretary may ask the trainer to remove any horse from the premises if it does not have a certain number of works within a set period.

Stand next to your trainer and let him point out an assortment of things to watch for. In addition to those under his care, he will recognize many of the other horses, not only by the identification on the saddle blankets but also from paying attention each day. Part of his job is to watch the competition. He may also be on the alert for quality mounts that he thinks would be worth claiming and adding to his stable. For now, you will want to try to follow the horses in your trainer's barn. It takes awhile to learn to keep your eye on them when they are on the far side. In time, you'll develop a better eye, which will help you even while watching races from the front side.

The trainer always carries a stopwatch to the workouts to monitor the progress of his wards. Have him tell you in advance what he is watching for. Each of these athletes is at a different stage of development. Some of the young ones aren't trying to set records. Their job is to learn to run under the control of their rider. Today may be a day for the horse to improve physical stamina or learn to pace itself until it's time to kick into high gear, or maybe even discover how to challenge competitors.

The experienced runners may be trying longer distances or going through their regular paces to keep in shape for the next contest. The trainer will have instructed his exercise riders as to how far he wants them to run their charges, and, if it is a timed workout, how hard to push it.

Of course, the best fun is to watch your horse work out. If your trainer knows which day you will be visiting, he will undoubtedly try to have at least one of your horses work that day. Not only will you get to see the speed and beauty of this would-be champion, but you'll also be able to discuss plans with the trainer. After the workout, the trainer and exercise rider will talk about how the horse handled any problems and what it seemed to like or not like. This data will be entered into the daily training book so that the next session can be modified to further sharpen the horse's skills.

After the morning workouts your trainer may suggest you take a break by going to the backside cafeteria for coffee or breakfast. Don't miss this opportunity. You'll meet fascinating people whose lifestyles vastly differ from your own. They often will share stories that are very entertaining to a newcomer. Jockeys, groomsmen, owners, vets, and track employees all see this game from slightly different perspectives. As your trainer introduces you around, you'll get a chance to make new friends. If you visit the backside periodically, these people will come to recognize and welcome you. It is here that you may first experience the feeling of entering your new world as the owner of a racing Thoroughbred.

As you watch your trainer interact, you'll see the importance of the network he has built. You'll also get to know all about horses, but not just yours. As these professionals share their experiences, you'll come to understand how each horse has its own personality, temperament, strengths, and weaknesses.

The track kitchen provides a central meeting place where deals are struck, problems are discussed, and horsemen sit and enjoy each other's company. It is also the best place to get to know the jockeys. They often sit in groups, enjoying coffee and just "shooting the bull" after the morning workouts. This is break time for them. But they are also interested in meeting new owners and trainers who may help their careers. It is among the most relaxed parts of their day.

The first time I ever visited the backside of a track, the trainer I was interviewing took me to the cafeteria and within an hour I had met Gary Stevens and talked briefly with Corey Nakatani about my becoming involved as an owner. On the West Coast these two are big-name jockeys! Their willingness to spend a few minutes chatting with me, even though they knew I was a novice just considering buying into my first horse, was a thrill.

A jockey's day begins at dawn as the jockeys come to the track to work the horses, and it isn't over until their last race of the day. For tracks that run in the afternoon, this means by seven in evening. They have little time for sleep and less for leisure. And although virtually every jockey in the world rides horses for the love of it, this is also a business. It isn't pleasure riding.

When they arrive at the track, the first priority for experienced jockeys is to work the horses of trainers with whom they have a contract. They must also develop relationships with other trainers for whom they may like to ride. If a jockey is fortunate enough to start winning races, he or she will build a reputation and will have no problem getting assigned rides.

For jockeys who are just starting out and those still getting established, this networking with new people is far more important. They must find those owners and trainers who will give them a chance. And to do that, they must develop relationships. The money for exercising horses is almost negligible, but the networking is critical.

Lunch With the Experts

If you go to the backside periodically, you'll soon begin running into people you know. When you are introduced to interesting people, swap phone numbers and ask if they would be willing to have lunch with you. Some owners and trainers will surely have a horse running in one of the races that day and you can help cheer on their mount. You'll be surprised at how exciting and fulfilling that can be once you know the people involved.

You'll also come to understand the importance of certain races for particular jockeys. When you see them add a meaningful victory, a word of congratulations will endear you to them. In less time than you think, you'll no longer be seen as a novice but will be considered part of the inner circle.

As this entire day has been set aside to be at the track, use each hour constructively. When you set up the appointment with your trainer to visit the backside, see if there is someone he knows that would be interesting for you to get acquainted with. He may have other owners joining him or her at his barn that day, or he might ask a business associate to have lunch with you and help you understand the racing business from another angle. Think how much you could learn from spending an hour with a vet, a farrier, a track official, or whomever.

Don't be shy. If you see other owners standing at the backside watching their horses, go over and introduce yourself. Let them know this is your first shot at being a horseman and ask them to tell you how they got involved. Ask about their horses, their trainer, and so on. You'll find yourself coming away from almost every conversation with at least one or two new ideas.

Countless friendships have begun at the track, where people have shared their experience and love for the horses. So put away your shyness and

reach out to other owners. It won't be long until someone with less experience than you is tapping on your shoulder and saying, "Mind if I ask you
a few questions?"

What about taking a jockey to lunch? That would be fun, right? Forget it!
Jockeys are paranoid about gaining weight. Most don't eat lunch. Or breakfast for that matter. And what they do eat for dinner would hardly keep a
cat alive. So it's best not to embarrass them with a dinner invitation. Enjoy
their company over coffee at the cafeteria and let them know of your regard
for their profession. They will appreciate your understanding and most
often be quite willing to help you learn more about horse racing.

Studying the Guides

There is a great deal to learn about handicapping races. A multitude of
books, pamphlets, and other help is available at the gift shop, as well as free
material from the track's information counters.

In all of life's endeavors, success and confidence come from rolling up
your sleeves and gaining firsthand experience. But this does not have to be
either risky or costly. If you are new to the world of racing, you will learn
and gain a great deal by spending the afternoon at the races, betting your
favorite choices. Here, learning to be a proficient handicapper isn't the
point. The need to predict which horse is most likely to win in each race will
also sharpen your thinking about ownership. You will have more riding on
your bets than the average fan because you are now looking at why each
owner thinks his or her horse can win in this race.

Studying the available guides will teach you far more than how to be a
better gambler. If you stay alert and watch for something more than making a little profit from your bet, you will learn much about individual horses. If there are ten races that day with an average of seven horses competing in each race, that equates to seventy animals for you to assess. How can
you do that? You certainly will not have enough time to think through the
issues between races; that's less than thirty minutes. If you haven't done
homework ahead of time, your efforts will be no more effective than betting on the jockey wearing the prettiest silks.

And by the way, do place a bet on each race. Bet small, if you like, but get some money down. Nothing will focus your attention more, or make the lesson stick, like having a vested interest. The lessons learned from studying the data are of a different sort than what you learn on the backside, and a combination of these lessons will make you a more successful owner.

Understand that the first time you try handicapping, the going will be slow. You'll have to learn to interpret each of the published guides, the symbols used, and where to find the most pertinent information. After you've done this a few times, it will become as easy for you as it is for a draftsman to read a blueprint or an electrician a schematic. Have you ever seen a blueprint or schematic? If you aren't a draftsman or an electrician, those documents look bewildering, as will the racing documents at first. The latter, however, are written and designed for ordinary people to use, so take heart; you just have to learn the signs and codes.

Using the Right Tools

So what are the factors that make a horse stand out against its peers? To begin with, you'll need to buy various publications, some of which you will purchase before going through the entrance gate and some after.

Just outside the entrance gates, vendors will be selling individual tip sheets, or tout sheets, for between three dollars and five dollars. Although you may never choose to use these again, you might want to buy one just to check it out.

After you've paid your admission fee, just inside the entrance gate and before you enter the clubhouse or grandstand, purchase 1) the daily program, (2) the *Daily Racing Form* (which looks like a newspaper), and, if you like, (3) the racing section of the local newspaper.

Daily Program

Each day, the local racing association publishes a program of races to be run that day. Again, take a few minutes to scan the entire program, page by page, to see all of what it contains. Many fans fail to do this and miss an array of opportunities, deals, and information that could be very helpful. Often free seminars are offered on ownership, handicapping, understanding conformation, and so on. You will also find listings of how the trainers and jockeys are faring in the meet, special entertainment programs offered after the racing day, and a variety of charts and instructions to aid in making the best possible bets.

Today, each fan (or in this case you, acting as handicapper) is looking for a bargain just like a new owner would in deciding which horse to purchase. That is, where could he put the least amount of money at risk for the greatest chance at making a profit? It is the development of that ability that distinguishes the successful handicapper. It does little good to bet on the preferred horse, as the odds aren't favorable. You've put your money at risk, and even if it comes in first, you win a pittance.

The daily program lists the horses by their post positions, which are determined at a drawing after all the horses have been entered in a race. The horses will be listed numerically, with horse number one entering the gate nearest the rail. If there is a double entry, representing a single betting interest (maybe the same owner or the same trainer), the second horse in the coupling will be represented by the same number as the first but followed with an "A." Look for an explanation of all the symbols at the front of the program.

The information listed under the horse's name in the program is important, and includes its age, color, gender, the state in which it was bred (that is to say, foaled), and its pedigree. Elsewhere, the program will list how jockeys and trainers participating in the meet are faring and also their year-to-date statistics. A good jockey, trainer, or successful combination can significantly impact the likelihood of winning.

Daily Racing Form

This publication has been around since 1894 and twenty-five regional editions are published every day of the year except for Christmas. Check out the *Form*'s web site at drf.com. You may also request a free guide or ask any other question about the *Form* by calling 800-306-FORM. The abbreviated explanation that follows will be nowhere near as complete as the guide provided by the publisher. Nonetheless, it should help you get started.

As you did with the other tools, first just flip through the pages to get an idea of the layout and what information is offered. On the front page, in the upper left-hand corner, is a list of the tracks and races covered in this issue. Industry news is covered in the first few pages, followed by race listings from the tracks included in that particular edition. Finally, just before the classified ads in the back, is a report on the latest workouts.

Note the different sections of the *Form*. You will find yourself referring to and using them on a regular basis. The summaries on the inside of the front page, the "Handicappers Page," "Selections," "Spot Plays," and so on are all tools that will help you see opportunities and better qualify your decisions.

Spending a couple of hours with this literature will acquaint you with each of the horses running. When race time arrives, you will no longer be looking at just a group of handsome animals but at individuals with a history. There are other things to watch for when you actually see them up close, but we'll cover that when discussing what to look for at the paddock.

Getting Acquainted with the Facilities

Okay, your homework is done and you are ready for some action, as well as a good stretch of the legs. If this is your first visit to a particular racing facility, spend thirty minutes getting acquainted with the layout.

Penny Chenery, the owner of the now-deceased champion Secretariat, relates a common frustration in *The Blood-Horse* video *Owning Thoroughbreds*. "When you walk into a racetrack, there is no arrow that says, 'go here.' There's no place that says, 'this way to the track.' You don't know how to bet, you don't really know what you're there for, and you have to be prepared to be the tourist and ask dumb questions. I didn't know what a claiming race was, I didn't know what the fractions were because the race trackers talk in sort of a telegraphese (sic) system. They talk about the time of a work in a minute and two. Well, what?"

She goes on to offer some encouragement to the meek. "There are so many things that you just don't know, and you've got to treat it as an adventure, as if you've gone to a foreign country and this is a new language and it doesn't come with a very good guidebook. Just go along and pick up the lingo as you can. Everybody has gone through this process the first time they went to the track unless they went with a relative or someone who taught them as they went. Reading the *Racing Form* takes time to understand but it's worth it."

Most people feel overwhelmed the first time they go to the racetrack. The goal is to learn your way around and get rid of the neophyte heebie-jeebies as quickly as possible. Do this at a time when you aren't in a hurry.

Go back to the clubhouse entrance. Find the window where you may purchase a reserved seat. The grandstand area also has a similar window. Some people like having a seat they know is theirs. Many others, however, enjoy wandering around and may sit in one place for a while and then move to another non-reserved seat. When you sit in the non-reserved section, if you leave a newspaper, or some other item of little value on the seat, others will (at least most of the time) understand that you plan to return.

Walk around and notice where all the restaurants, restrooms, and betting windows are. Also keep your eyes open for the entrance to the more exclusive turf club. It is doubtful that you will be visiting there today, but should a member invite you, don't miss the opportunity. The furnishings, artwork, betting windows, and even the restrooms are the finest in the building. This is the only area in which a dress code is enforced. So if invited, be sure to ask about attire. The normal minimum required for gentlemen is jacket and tie, and the ladies may be wearing anything from elegantly casual to knock-your-socks-off fashions.

If there are wealthy or famous people in attendance that day, the turf club is the place you would probably see them. And if you plan to spend a lot of time at a particular track and are willing to pay the price, you can apply for membership. Many turf clubs have lengthy waiting lists, and it may take years for your name to reach the top.

The grandstand is akin to a general admission area, not offering as many frills while still providing everything needed for a day of racing and betting. Fans can see the horses just as clearly, but the eating areas will not be as plush or well placed as in the clubhouse.

Ask for the location of the general information booth and check out all the free literature. The booth will offer a number of brochures with instructions on how to place a bet, schedules for classes and seminars, and much more. The attendants are used to first-time visitors, so don't be afraid to ask questions. Ask for a layout of the track facility.

On the layout map you can see that the grandstand seating (as you face the track) is positioned to the left of the finish line, and the clubhouse area is roughly from the finish line to the right. The grandstand is usually one and a half times larger than the clubhouse. At some tracks a tunnel may provide access to the infield, where there may be additional entertainment or viewing. Families with children might prefer to picnic and let the kids run around in this casual setting.

Next, enter the seating area of the grandstand and go to the highest floor available and check it out. The vantage from there differs significantly from the first or second floor. See what the track looks like from the extreme edges, as well as near the finish line. After that, walk out to the track and stand by the rail for a different perspective. Then follow the rail to the gap where the horses enter the track from the paddock. Right next to that path, on the grandstand side, is the winner's circle. One day, hopefully, you will have your picture taken there with your winning horse and jockey.

As you go back into the grandstand, find out where the paddock is and how you get to it. Walk around it while there are only a few people present

The Turf Club entrance to Hollywood Park.

and become familiar with its layout. You will want to make the trip to this saddling area before betting on each race.

Once the races have begun, experience watching the races from the various viewpoints. You may find that your preferred place to observe is not right at the finish line. And everyone should have the experience, at least once, of standing at the rail as eight or ten of those thousand-pound animals come thundering past at breakneck speed. Some fans, known as "railbirds," don't want to watch from anywhere else.

As you have already done your homework and will be getting up frequently to look at the horses between races, you won't need a reserved seat. Of course, if it makes you feel more comfortable to have your own spot, go ahead and buy one. Once you have found your reserved seat, look around to know just where you are in relation to all the places you'll want to go to after the crowd arrives.

You will now feel free to move without confusion about where you are and where you want to go. Select the handiest restrooms, restaurants, and betting areas. Your mind can now stay focused on the races and making decisions that can win you money.

Afternoon/Evening at the Races

Okay, it's just about time for the first race. Before you head for your seat, prepare for an active experience. There's a lot more fun waiting for you than just sitting in the stands and watching the horses go around. Much of the enjoyment of being at the track is missed if all you do is place a bet and root for your horse to win.

About twenty minutes before each race, the trainers and grooms will bring the horses to the paddock. Make your way there before every race to look at the horses before you bet on them. Go early to establish a good vantage point. It is essential to get a reading on how each horse seems to feel just before the race. Furthermore, the best assessment you will get is before the horses are saddled and the jockeys are on their backs.

You can tell a lot by watching how a horse behaves just prior to a race. Most of these horses have gone through this process many times, and they know they are about to race. They have known it since the early morning, as they will have gotten a different amount of feed and will have been treated differently on the day of a race. So they are "wired." Remember that horses like to run. They love to run. Can't wait to run. They feel the same adrenaline rush as a human athlete when he approaches a race or athletic competition. They are jazzed.

In his book, *Dirt Road to the Derby*, trainer Bob Baffert tells about watching a horse "on the walk" to the paddock to see if he is calm and ready. "Silver Charm looked great. Nothing bothered or excited him. One thing about this horse, he is so cool. He's got ice water in his veins. I looked up and I saw one of the contenders, Pulpit, and he was doing the Mexican hat dance in front of us. He was jumping and rearing and getting all hot. I could see all these horses falling apart in front of me, and Silver Charm was quiet and relaxed. I told my brothers, 'I hope he's not getting a temperature on me right now.'

"But as soon as he made the turn to go into the tunnel, he started to coil a little and flex his muscles. When he does that, I know he's on. I said, 'I like that. That's a good sign.' "

As the horses are led into the paddock, look for a fire in their eyes coupled with a centered attitude. Some of them may be a bit hard to handle, but that doesn't mean the horse is ornery. Rather, it's that adrenaline rush, the spit-and-vinegar we talk about that's surfacing. It is not a good sign, however, if they seem to be out of control.

The pre-race routine is always the same. As the horses are brought into the paddock area, a track official will check the tattoo under each horse's upper lip. This ensures that this is the horse scheduled for that race. The horse identifier will also be checking other markings, but all that will happen so quickly you won't notice a thing.

Once the identifier has allowed the horse into the paddock, the horse may be led around the ring and then taken to the stall bearing the same number as its post position. It will be saddled and then walked around the ring one or more times, until the call for "riders up." Once more it will be led around the ring, this time with the jockey mounted, and then out through the gap to the track.

As the horses emerge onto the track, the trumpeter sounds the familiar

"Call to Post." The time in the paddock area goes quickly but will give you an opportunity to look at the horses before they set out to the starting gate.

In that brief time, what should you be watching for? You've already gone over the statistics and have marked those horses you believe may have a statistical edge. The racing secretary has designed this race so all the contenders have a shot at winning, possibly giving allowances to some and handicaps to others.

If your pick is running at a greater distance than ever before, you may pay special attention to its conformation. Does it have the length of body that will provide a stride to compete with the others? Of the horses you have selected, how do they carry themselves? Often, a horse with an arched neck that prances is indicating that it's ready. Maybe the horse you thought strong is walking around the ring as if bored or tired, head hanging down and listless. Are you still ready to put money on it? The way a horse moves its ears can indicate a great deal. An alert horse will move its ears as it listens to the

Watch the behavior of horses in the paddock.

A horse identifier checks the entrant's lip tattoo.

crowd, paying attention to what's going on without acting spooked.

Almost all trainers say they prefer high-energy horses with quick minds and clear eyes but that also have a calm, even disposition. When you find those qualities in the horses you examine, it may be time to rethink where to put your money. Allow your impressions to affect your judgment, even at the last minute. Certainly you don't want to negate all the statistical research you did earlier, but watching the horses as they are saddled can give you just the edge you need to make the right decision, particularly if you couldn't decide between two that looked good on paper.

As you might imagine, the best experience you'll ever have at the paddock occurs when one of your own horses is running. You may have seen other owners standing there, talking with their trainer and jockey as last-minute instructions are given. Someday, when it's your turn to whisper an encouraging word to the horse and offer the thumbs up to the jockey, the excitement is unbelievable. For now, however, note the behavior of the horses you have just observed and head for your seat. You have one more step to take before you make your financial commitment.

Settled at your home base for the afternoon, the final bit of information you need is right in front of you: the tote board. Erected directly across the racing track from the stands, this electronic billboard gives you the actual odds based on how people are betting on the horses. The odds will change every few seconds as the computers tally how much money is being placed on which horse. This is the nature and excitement of pari-mutuel wagering. You are not betting against the house or those who own the racetrack, but against those others gathered in the stands and at off-track betting parlors, pitting their wits against you. All you have to do is make better choices than the majority and you go home a winner.

If you are looking to capitalize on a likely winner with really good odds, you must pay attention to the actual odds immediately preceding each race. Professional handicappers don't go to the window and place their bets until just before the race begins. The reason is that sometimes the odds will change noticeably at the last minute. If either your wager, or the amount of your wager, is based on the odds offered, you may change your mind at the last minute, too. Watching for this will make you a more profitable handicapper. Just for kicks, next to the printed morning-line odds make a note in your program of the odds just as the horses are being loaded

The post parade.

into the starting gate. It is enlightening. One more note, if your own horse is running in this particular race, there is nothing to decide. It is against the rules of racing for an owner or trainer to bet on any other horse when his horse is racing. And who, besides a crook, would want to?

It's time to make your decision and put your money on the line. As soon as the horses have paraded past the fans on their way to the starting gate, you should head for the betting windows. Sometimes the lines are long. You also may get behind someone with an entire list of exotic wagers who will dominate the window forever. Someone once advised me never to stand in line behind a woman with a big purse. What that has to do with anything I still don't have a clue, but I always keep an eye out, just in case.

Back at your seat you have every reason to be hopeful. You've done your homework and made a wager based on a good rationale. There is no guarantee that you will win, but you are several steps ahead of the majority you're betting against.

Okay. We've spent time in this chapter discussing what it is like for a handicapper to attend a race, assess the field of horses, and make a decision on where to put his money. This book, however, is geared toward helping you think like an owner of one of those horses. Do you see how the same research and mental process are required of every owner before entering a horse into a given race?

Each horse in every race has potential, a history, and a chance. It only makes sense to put your horse into a competition where it has a chance to win and where it can develop its skills as it matures. This is the reason some owners and trainers want to wait to see what other horses are placed in a race before deciding to enter the competition. It doesn't make sense to enter your horse into a race in which it has little chance of winning.

The minimal risk the handicapper puts down at the betting window is a much smaller bet than the one you make with your trainer when you decide to enter your horse in a competition. But you now know much more about what to look for when you scan the condition book and consider your options. If you play this game smart, not taking bigger chances than you can afford, you will surely have your times of standing in the winner's circle with your horse and your team.

10

A Day at the Farm

Whether or not you ever invest in breeding stock, plan to visit at least a couple of farms. Every owner finds it an eye-opening experience.

To prepare for a visit to a horse farm, read the book *Country Life Diary* by Josh Pons. In the early 1990s Pons was commissioned by *The Blood-Horse* magazine to write a three-year diary of running a breeding farm. That diary ran as a series in the magazine and was later published as a book, now in its second printing. *Country Life Diary* (The Blood-Horse, Inc. 1992) makes you feel as if you have actually witnessed breeding, foaling, and other aspects of a working horse farm.

It will also trigger questions for your visit. Jot those things down, and your visit will be more meaningful.

Horse farms welcome visits from prospective horse owners, provided you set up an appointment. Even if you drive by a farm that looks lazy and quiet, understand that beyond the apparent tranquility, horse farms are busy. Employees won't be able to stop their work to show you around unless they're prepared.

As you plan your visit to the horse farm, remember it is not an occasion to entertain small children. The average horse

The setting for **Country Life Diary.**

weighs a half-ton, and although most are quite tame, Thoroughbreds are not pets. Quick movements spook horses. And what child does not move and jump around quickly? There is a time to introduce children to the joy of being around horses, but this is not that time. It not only can be dangerous but can also detract from what you can learn.

Also, though horse farms are much cleaner than most people imagine, you still may have to climb some fences or walk through muddy areas. Dress casually and wear walking shoes that can be easily cleaned.

Wide Open Spaces

For city folks, it is surprising to learn that there is seldom a foul smell on a horse farm unless it happens to be the season for fertilizing the fields. Instead, the air is so crisp and clean you'd think you were in the woods. As you step out of your car, indulge yourself. Take in a few deep breaths, allow your metabolism to slow down, and relax into the pastoral atmosphere.

When you enter the office at a small farm, the office manager may be the only one to greet you. The atmosphere will be very casual. Just "pull up a chair and sit a spell." No matter how casual it may appear, however, if this farm has been around awhile you can bet everything gets done and done well. Horse farm owners rise early and often put in a day of heavy manual labor, yet they can be extremely laid back, appearing to have no pressure or deadlines to meet.

At a large horse farm, several people may be on the staff. One of them may ask you to sign in and then usher you into a conference room. Don't let that formality worry you. You're not in for a sales pitch that concludes with lawyers bearing contracts. The purpose of that meeting is just to get acquainted and allow your host to get to know exactly what you want to see and if there is anything specific with which he or she can help you.

On a large farm, the director of guest relations may show you around. These professionals are outgoing, articulate, and make excellent hosts or hostesses. They are also remarkably knowledgeable. Many have worked for years on a horse farm, and some have college degrees in equine husbandry. A good plan is to visit at least one smaller and one larger farm.

Whether accompanied by the farm manager or a staff member, once you leave the office, a horse farm is a horse farm. All breeding farms are designed with similar objectives. And even on a small farm, you'll cover a lot of ground. As you set out, keep in mind the logic of the horse farm layout. Each paddock or pasture is assigned a certain category of horse and so are the barns. As you are escorted to a given area, consider where it is situated and how it relates to the others. Soon you'll have a sense for the whole.

Although each host will show off his or her operation differently, you will be introduced to each area of the horse farm in a logical sequence. The stallions will be in a separate area. They will stay quieter if kept at a distance from the females to reduce the enticement. The broodmares and fillies will be sectioned off into one or more paddock areas. The young ones are also grouped by age: weanlings in one area, yearlings in another.

Ask questions. How many acres comprise the farm, what makes this farm unique, and what is the strategy or plan that governs the farm? You will learn how many horses reside there and their general value. Almost every horse farm prides itself on the stallions that stand there. The hosts will all recount the superstars bred or foaled under their supervision. You will be surprised at how well these people know all their animals. They

Horses are grouped by gender, age, or both.

seem to remember the name, history, and pedigree of every horse on the farm, almost as if it were part of their extended family.

It stands to reason that if this is a breeding farm, you will hear of breeding specifics in candid terms. Be prepared to hear about these issues. This is another reason not to have children with you. It might be awkward or embarrassing for either you or your host if he or she goes into detail surpassing the scope of your child's understanding.

At each point of the breeding process, things can go wrong. Some stallions are not as fertile as others, and some broodmares do not get pregnant easily. A variety of strategies must be used to help mares become and stay pregnant. Sometimes mares lose their foals or may deliver one that is deformed. When the foal is not positioned correctly in the birth canal, the delivery can be terribly hard. The host will share these stories as you walk and talk together. Feel free to ask questions or seek explanations of how he or she handles the difficulties that occur.

It is fascinating to consider the ways farm employees use their ingenuity

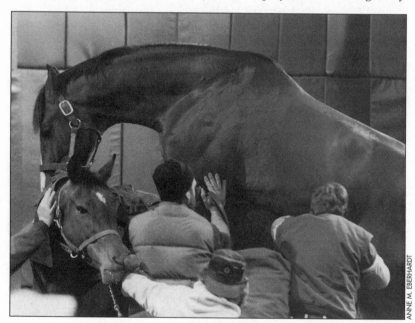

In the breeding shed.

as they coax these animals into being productive. Not all breeding takes place just "doin' what comes naturally." To protect their horses, farmers employ unusual tactics to bring about a successful mating. To expedite or make intercourse safe, they often handle the animals in ways surprising to the uninitiated. For instance, a mare may not be ready to accept the attention of the stallion.

A mare goes into heat, or estrus, on a cycle of every eighteen or so days and stays in heat for about four days. At that time she's very receptive to a stallion. The moment she's out of heat, however, she is really out of heat and will not tolerate a male around her. It's especially touchy when a filly or mare is bred for the first time. These bewildered virgins aren't sure what is happening. Even though they are physiologically ready, they are afraid. At either of those times, the females may become violent. Stallions are very expensive animals and a well-placed kick could cripple or kill him. That's why teasers are used.

This unlucky horse has the job of sidling up to the mare and teasing her. It's not so bad if a fence or partition keeps the teaser and mare separated to avoid an accidental coupling. Some farms allow the teaser into the pasture with the mares and two or three employees will be right there to interrupt the process, although this is not the most common practice.

Once the mare has proved ready to breed, the lucky stallion will be unlikely to get hurt when it's his turn.

After coitus, sperm stay active for forty-eight to seventy-two hours. The vet will use ultrasound to see whether the mare is pregnant and will look for a positive result within two weeks. If she is not pregnant, the mare is bred again the following month. It is not unusual for a mare to be covered a number of times before a pregnancy is confirmed. Therefore, when a mare is sent to a certain stallion, she may stay at the farm for several weeks until pregnancy is confirmed.

Breeders tell interesting stories of what's done to get one animal coupled with another. What does one do if alignment is a problem when joining a tall mare and shorter stallion? A variety of solutions may be employed, including bringing the horses to a steep hill to mate or building a platform for the purpose.

As the stallion prepares to mount the mare, several employees work together. One will hold onto the mare's halter in one hand and possibly one of her lifted front legs in the other. This is so she will not be able to get a strong footing for kicking, if she had a mind to. They then place a leather blanket, or shield, over her neck so when the stallion is in the throes of passion and bites her neck to gain a better purchase, he won't injure her. Another person, called the "pilot," will wash the stallion's penis both before and after mating and will help guide it into the mare. The entire process takes only a few minutes, but as you can see, one question about "what do you do in that case?" leads to another, and you'll be glad you left the kids at home while you get your own tutoring.

Visiting a horse farm at any time of the year is enjoyable and educational, but you may find a more relaxed setting in either the late summer or early fall. The foaling season is over by then, and the owner and his staff will be more rested. Hosting visitors is easier now.

A horse farm's calendar can be thought of in two parts: the breeding and foaling season that begins approximately in February and goes through

Mares and foals enhance the scenery.

June, and attendance at the sales and auctions that take place in spring, summer, and fall when horses will be sold and new stock purchased.

The mating and foaling season is high pressure. Vans bring in mares that need attention as they settle into their new environment. During the day, scheduled breedings of any number of stallions must be supervised and fully documented. During those same months most of the pregnant mares will give birth during the night hours. The mares that are approaching their due date must be monitored around the clock. And when labor begins, it's time to get out of bed. Often weeks go by with little opportunity for a full night's rest. And lest we forget the dedication required; this goes on for five long months.

Add to all this activity volumes of paperwork that must accompany a carefully overseen Thoroughbred operation. Every injection or medical procedure, every mating attempt, and every birth must be recorded as part of the permanent file of each animal. Photographs are taken, hair samples for DNA testing, and every possible marking on the young horse must be recorded to ensure its identity. Consequently, February through June is an exhausting time for the staff, each taking a deep breath in preparation and giving a huge sigh of relief at the conclusion.

At the seasonal auctions, the horse farms take cash from sold inventory and put it into promising new stock. Owners and breeders must select which sales are right for individual stock. For instance, one sale may be specifically for yearlings or two-year-olds. Another may be a select sale, at which the horses included have been screened for quality. Yet another may offer mixed stock. The breeder uses his experience and hopes for a bit of luck in placing his stock in the "right" sale. If successful, those decisions may increase the value of his horse farm.

The Stallion Barn

The first area you are likely to be shown is the stallion barn. Stallions are the mainstay upon which a horse farm's reputation is built. Note the difference in temperament among stallions, mares, and young horses. Stallions not only are more aggressive but are also significantly bigger. Although most are not mean, some are so violent they appear to be insane.

In chapter 3 we discussed how a stallion's value might range from several hundred thousand dollars into the millions. Some have sold for $20 million to $30 million. Out of all the thousands of males with perfect pedigrees and out of the hundreds with winning racing careers, only a proportional few will be considered to sire a new line of offspring. That is why they are so valuable and why stallions are the pride of a horse farm.

Managing a stallion's career is tricky work. There are many options available to mare owners, so the stallion manager must advertise and get the word out about how successful his stallions are as sires of new winners. The stud fee must be considered reasonable (if not a bargain), and the horse must be able to impregnate mares with consistency.

Another consideration in stallion management is how many coverings prove optimum. Do you always want to sell as many seasons as possible? Not necessarily. A 1998 article in *The Blood-Horse* magazine reported, "If you own a stallion, every season sold means more money to the bottom line. It

The grandeur of stallion barns can reflect the value of the occupants.

also means more chances for your stallion to have a leading runner. If you own a broodmare that produces stakes-winning offspring, it means more opportunity to breed to the stallion of your choice. It also means having your mare produce a foal that has a better chance of being by a sire that has a top runner. Then again, for the stallion owner, it's tough to have good percentage statistics when you have more foals. And it's harder to be among the standout yearlings when there are so many more by a sire."

Once you understand the money involved and the implications of each factor in the breeding process, you will come to respect these rare producers. Horse farms will do everything possible to ensure that the stallions, and all other stock, stay healthy and happy and are not endangered or aggravated in any way.

It is dumbfounding what simple things can threaten a stallion's welfare: children causing a commotion as they walk past the paddocks to school, adolescents throwing stones or bottles, or the neighbor's barking dog. Even such a simple thing as a young deer jumping the pasture fence may spook the horses. Once horses are startled, they may run blindly into an obstruction or a wire, possibly getting crippled or even having to be euthanized. Horse farm employees keep a close eye on these seemingly trivial annoyances as they can create stunning damage.

Broodmares and Fillies

Broodmares and fillies will be the most docile and approachable of all the horses you encounter. Pregnant mares and often the fillies are kept in paddocks together. Having just visited the stallion barn, you will find these horses seem refreshingly calm and gentle. Although some can be cantankerous and many are still quite young and frolic in the pasture, you will notice that the mothers-in-waiting, in particular, lose a little of their mischievousness.

Notice how the mares differ in appearance throughout their pregnancy. Because the foaling season is from January through May, depending on the time of year you visit the farm, the mares are likely to be "showing" more obviously toward year-end.

The peak month in nature's calendar for mating seems to be in April. As all Thoroughbreds are considered a year older on January 1, regardless of their actual birth month, those who oversee the breeding of these animals have to make a few adjustments.

April's longer hours of daylight apparently signal to the mare that it is springtime, and her system kicks into gear preparing for motherhood. To extend that breeding season and limit the months the foals will be born, man has learned to trick the mare into believing April has arrived much earlier.

The breeder accomplishes this by enclosing the mares in stalls and controlling the lighting so their internal time clock is fooled. This causes the mares to be more receptive to mating from as early as February to as late as June. Their eleven-month gestation then produces foals in the early part of the following year so that by their first birthday in January they will be as physically developed as possible.

Weanlings and Yearlings

Finally, you'll visit the section where the younger horses are kept. Even from half a mile away, these are the easiest to identify. Like children of any species, they run and dance, skip and frolic.

A baby horse is called a foal from the time it's born until it is weaned, approximately six months after its birth. From the time it is weaned until its first birthday, it is a weanling.

All Thoroughbreds are considered a year older on January 1. On that date, weanlings become yearlings, yearlings become two-year olds, and so forth. The physical differences among weanlings, yearlings, and two-year-olds are substantial. It is during this relatively short period that buying for quick resale and profit, called pinhooking, takes place. It is also during these early stages of their lives that being born early or late in the foaling season is apparent. Though they might be considered the same age, horses born early in the season will usually have more developed musculature and fluidity. Because their racing careers begin when they are two, this development has a great deal to do with the price they command at an auction.

Check whether these young horses are shod. At some horse farms, "summer shoes" are worn to keep hooves in good shape and to keep them from splitting. Horses can crack their hooves by doing nothing more than stomping their feet to chase flies off their legs. A prospective buyer, however, may consider shoes on a very young horse to be a bad sign, as shoes are sometimes used to correct deformities in a young pigeon-toed or knock-kneed horse.

Even in humans, sometimes an infant may be born with a foot angled either out or in. The easiest time to correct bone alignment is during early growth spurts, before bones solidify into permanent shape. A pediatrician may suggest setting the foot in a cast to help correct that flaw in nature before the bones set and the child develops an unnatural or cumbersome gait.

To keep this from happening to a horse, an experienced farrier may design a shoe that will encourage the bone to develop more on one side than the other. This helps nature to correct a weakness before the bone is set and allows the animal to move more freely with a natural movement.

Another, more invasive, procedure, also used to correct early deformities, is called periosteal stripping — a minor but controversial surgical procedure. As it does not cut into or alter the natural bone structure or joints of a young

A foal is considered a foal until it is weaned.

horse, it does not have to be recorded or declared in the Thoroughbred's medical history. Some owners take exception to applying any procedure that might affect what nature has produced. Nevertheless, Thoroughbred industry officials have not found fault with, or required documentation of, either trimming or stripping. Should this ever come up within your partnership, you will want to discuss the implications with your managing partner to determine his or her opinion on this controversial subject.

If you own a young horse, you will have a number of options as it matures. You may decide to keep that foal until it reaches the track and can compete. Who knows, you may have a stakes winner that will open exciting possibilities for you. Alternatively, you may sell it privately or offer it

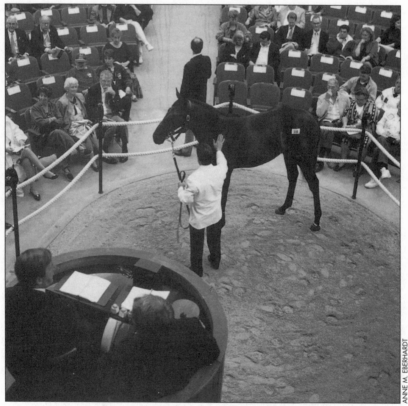

Selling a young horse at auction is one option.

for auction as a weanling, a yearling, or a two-year-old in training. The longer you keep it, the more it will show its maturity, muscle development, and potential. At an auction, that can multiply your investment several times over.

As you are shown around the horse farm, your host will repeatedly recount that, "this yearling is by the stallion so-and-so and out of its dam so-and-so." You'll hear this a lot because that is what initially defines the value of the horse. It is the pedigree that first makes a Thoroughbred a Thoroughbred. As you meet experienced horsemen, you'll find that many of them know the pedigrees of horses for several generations back. You do not need to memorize all this, but you will need the help and experience of people who can explain the implications of pedigree and racing history in any horse you consider buying. It is the first element suggesting the value of your investment before the horse has shown any physical promise and before the racing begins.

The Business Aspect of a Farm

As you walk around a horse farm, it is easy to forget it is a business. After all, with all this tranquility surrounding you who wants to think about money? The owner, however, must make a profit or he or she will be washed up in short order. He or she cannot afford to have horses that don't contribute to the bottom line. Every decision and policy on the horse farm is made with a view of turning a profit. Each of the areas you will have just visited, as well as each type of horse, represents an area of either profit or loss.

When you visit a horse farm and consider whom you want to partner with from this side of the business, you'll be looking for those people who run a profitable enterprise.

As you walk the farm, if you like what you see, declare from the onset where your interests lie. If you are considering an interest in a broodmare or stallion, or would like to buy a younger horse and watch it grow, say so. It will help your host understand what to explain in detail, and he will be better able to point out the rewards. If you keep him completely in the dark, he might skip over something of particular importance to you.

It is very unlikely that the farm owner or manager will try to twist your arm or jack up the price like a used car salesmen. It is in his best interest to identify where you best fit. If you are in the wrong partnership, it's not likely that you will remain a partner for very long. If you have a limited budget and aren't yet sure in which area you are best suited, let the owner or manager know that. If he understands the level of involvement you are considering and the amount of risk you can stand, he can make a much more realistic recommendation.

At the end of your farm visit, remember that a few compliments would be well received. If you like the way the horse farm looks, if the horses impress you, if you find your host to be particularly helpful and knowledgeable, say so. He will appreciate your kind words. When you get home, send a thank-you card with a few comments of what the visit meant to you. You may be starting a relationship with someone you'll be in business with for a long time.

11

A Day at the Auction

If the partnership you've joined, or the one you've started, is about to acquire a horse, it can do so in several ways. The partnership can buy one it likes directly from the owner, breed its own, or select one from a claiming race. Most Thoroughbreds, however, are sold at auction. It is the fastest and fairest determination of an animal's value.

The fair market value of any asset is defined as what a willing buyer will pay a willing seller at a given point. That is precisely what the auction provides: buyers, sellers, and horses all gathered to do business. No matter which auction you attend, hundreds of horses will be sold each day. Some will sell for less than a thousand dollars. Others will attract millions.

Don Blazer, in his book *Make Money With Horses* (Success Is Easy 1998), says "...there is usually a greater margin for profit when purchasing the horse through a sale. For one thing, it is much less costly to you to have a number of horses to choose from in a central location. Secondly, you have no personal experience in constructing a catalog page. Thirdly, you must be more astute when buying privately since you are relying entirely on your own knowledge and judgment. Most owners and breeders overestimate the value of their horses, and consequently ask more for them than they would bring at a sale. At a sale you also have the consensus of opinion to backup your appraisal and that is a big plus. Seldom will 20 or more other professional horsemen overbid a horse. When the bidding stops, that's about what the horse is worth."

Whether you buy your horse privately or at a public sale, it is very important that you learn to read a catalog page.

The Catalog Page

Every sale's catalog contains a page of information on each horse being auctioned. This information includes its pedigree and its racing history (if it has raced) and that of its predecessors. Even if you buy a horse privately from an individual, something similar to a catalog page, known as a pedigree report, is still available. These reports can be purchased from several online services listed in the Resources section at the end of this book.

Tens of thousands of horses are sold at auction each year through more than forty different sales. Let's say you've decided that you want to buy a horse. Maybe you've put together a partnership, a pool of money, and have found a trainer. Where do you start looking for a horse at an auction? Knowing it is impossible to place a definitive dollar value on a horse that goes to the highest bidder, how do you find prospects that fit your criteria out of the hundreds that will be sold at a single auction? The answer is to do a thorough examination of the sales catalog before you head for the sales site.

In reality, it would be foolhardy to try this on your own without significant experience. Instead, you would strategize over a number of candidates with either your trainer and/or bloodstock agent. As discussed in chapter 5, the bloodstock agent is a professional who is very familiar with pedigrees, parental histories, nicks, conformation, and so on. You pay for his

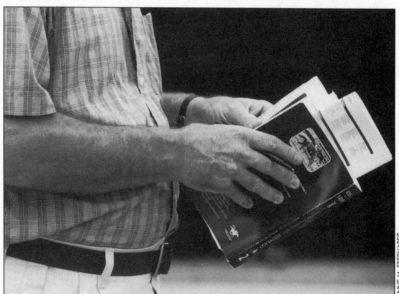

ANNE M. EBERHARDT

The catalog is a road map to a sale.

help, because an agent will know off the top of his head facts and data that would take you a great deal of time to research.

At the auction, you will want to examine the horse physically before making an offer or placing a bid, but before that time comes, you'll want to know as much as possible about the animal: its parentage, conformation, and history. Each of those factors will contribute to a ballpark value. Especially at an auction where dozens of horses meet your criteria, you want to limit the number of prospects to bid on. Therefore, go through the catalog of offerings to narrow the possibilities in advance.

The auction house will send a free catalog to anyone who requests one. Although they come in different sizes, they usually look like a thick paperback. In addition to the introductory section and statement of rules and policies that will govern the auction, the book dedicates one page for each horse offered. A "hip number" is attached to each horse for identification, when it is consigned to the sale. Some of the young horses have not yet been named and will simply be listed as a chestnut colt or a bay filly. In the various indices, you can track down horses for sale that were sired by a certain stallion or produced from a specific mare. Parentage dramatically affects sales price.

Along with your advisers, your job is first to identify as many candidates as possible that fall within your criteria. Next, weed that list down to a manageable number for you to see when you attend the sale. After a physical examination of the horses, you will come up with a short list of those you would be willing to bid upon, and of course, the top figure you would offer for each one. This process takes a lot of time, and your bloodstock agent's help will be much appreciated. He can do most of the grunt work for you, so when you attend the auction you will already have a list of prospects and can focus on narrowing it down to the short list.

Remember that your list needs to be long enough to still have candidates if you are outbid on earlier prospects. Sometimes you'll be disappointed that you weren't able to get the one you really wanted, but that is the nature of an auction. Have several prospects that if you get them at your own price will satisfy your quest for a bargain. Then you can go home happy.

Let's look at a few examples of catalog pages. The sale we will consider is the 2002 Fasig-Tipton Kentucky winter mixed sale that was held February 11-12 in Lexington. To start with, let's look at a young horse that has not yet raced. (See next page.)

This colt without a name is listed as "Bay Colt." Young horses that have not yet raced are normally not named, especially if they are sale horses. It will, therefore, simply be listed by its pedigree, color, gender, and foaling date. Throughout the auction, however, everyone will refer to horses by their hip number.

Start by analyzing the horse's pedigree. At the top of the page, a graphic summary puts forth the family tree of each horse for three generations.

Its sire (or father), Tale of the Cat, is listed in the next column to the right and on top. The dam (or mother), Debs Angel, is listed below the sire along with the year she was born. That is so you can see how old she is. She might be an unproven young broodmare, she might represent "the ol' gray mare," or she might lie somewhere between with offspring that may have already established a racing record. In the next columns you can then examine the parents of both the sire and dam, and then the great-grandparents of this sales prospect.

This colt, Hip Number 5, turned out to be the top-selling young horse at the auction. Anyone familiar with pedigree lines and racing records will immediately recognize the outstanding parentage just by looking at this top graphic. If you are not a big spender and are looking to find a bargain, you would pass on this colt. Still, he's an excellent example of what to look for on a catalog page, as a great deal more is revealed in a prospect like this as compared with one of lesser heritage.

Mares are often bred to a particular stallion in an attempt to meld strengths or eliminate weaknesses. As you get to know more about pedigrees, you will also expect to see certain traits and body structure reflected, or "thrown-off," from past generations to the new generation. Here again is the main reason a new investor really needs a bloodstock agent or other professional to interpret why this mating was planned and its potential strength.

As this colt has not yet raced, we want to know about those in his family that have raced, and more importantly, won. The first paragraph under the graphic, all in bold type, provides abbreviated details about his sire,

Barn 2E

Consigned by Gainesway, Agent

Hip No.

5

Bay Colt

```
                                          ┌ Storm Bird
                       ┌ Storm Cat ........┤
         ┌ Tale of the Cat ......┤         └ Terlingua
         │             │         ┌ Mr. Prospector
Bay Colt ........┤     └ Yarn ............┤
  February 15, 2001    │               └ Narrate
         │                              ┌ Raise a Native
         │             ┌ Raise a Cup .......┤
         └ Debs Angel ........┤          └ Spring Sunshine
           (1986)     │              ┌ Bold Bidder
                      └ Good Groomer ......┤
                                      └ Doll Ina
```

By **TALE OF THE CAT** (1994), black type winner of 5 races in 9 starts, $360,900, King's Bishop S. [G2], 2nd Whitney H. [G1], 3rd Vosburgh S. [G1] twice. Half-brother to black type winners **Minardi** (to 3, 2001, hwt. in England and Ireland, Middle Park S. [G1], etc.), **Spunoutacontrol**. His first foals are 2-year-olds of 2002.

1st dam

DEBS ANGEL, by Raise a Cup. 8 wins, 3 to 5, $233,734, Orinda H. [L] (GG, $31,600), Half Moon S. (MED, $21,000), 2nd Breeders' Cup Weekend Delight S. (TP, $11,296), Trevose S. (PHA, $7,970), 3rd Miss Woodford Breeders' Cup H. (MTH, $5,841). Dam of 7 foals of racing age, including a 3-year-old of 2002, seven to race, 6 winners, including--
    Angel's Touch (f. by Prized). 6 wins at 3 and 4, 2001, $71,710.
    Spin n Win (f. by Private Account). 2 wins at 3, $39,530. Producer.
    Marnay (f. by Kris S.). Winner at 2 and 3, $32,275.

2nd dam

GOOD GROOMER, by Bold Bidder. 3 wins at 2 and 4. Dam of 6 winners, incl.--
    DEBS ANGEL (f. by Raise a Cup). Black type winner, see above.
    GOOD BID (c. by Verbatim). 4 wins at 3, $101,190, Lexington H.-**G2**.
    Exactly E. 14 wins, 3 to 7, $95,124.
    Good and Cold. 16 wins, 5 to 13, $57,437.
    Jetsetter's Dream. Winner at 3, $21,095. Dam of 4 winners, incl.--
    ‖ Never Close. 7 wins, 2 to 6, 2001, $111,547.
    Neatness. Placed. Producer. G'dam of **MRSCOPPOLASKITCHEN**
    ‖ (f. by Regal Search) at 2, 2001, $36,400, Mom's Command S., etc.
    Groomed for Glory. Dam of 6 winners, including--
    Circle View Drive. 6 wins, 3 to 6, $128,460.

3rd dam

DOLL INA, by Helioscope. 13 wins, 3 to 6, $134,429, Margate H., 2nd New New York H., Margate H., 3rd Gallorette S., etc. Half-sister to **Whistling Kettle**. Dam of 3 winners, including--
    Lord Layabout. 2 wins at 3 in France; 3 wins, $25,113 in N.A., 3rd
    ‖ Canadian Turf H.-**G3**. Sire.
    Swinging Doll. Unraced. Dam of 4 winners, including--
    ‖ **AFFILIATE**. 9 wins, $373,124, Monmouth Invitational H.-**G1**, Vosburgh
    ‖ H.-**G2**, Jamaica H., Sport Page H., 2nd Swaps S.-**G1**, etc. Sire.
    ‖ **Ragtime Girl**. 4 wins, $53,445, 2nd Carmel H. Dam of **ENTITLED**
    ‖ **TO** [G2] ($489,281). Granddam of **FUSAICHI AIREDALE** (in Japan).
    ‖ My Light Fantastic. Placed. Dam of **To Little J D** ($100,424).
    Elly To. Unraced. Dam of **TOA FALCON** (Keio Hai Spring Cup [G2], etc.).

Breeders' Cup nominated.
KTDF.

12-01

Tale of the Cat. It always begins, "By so-and-so." Remember that horsemen always say "by" when they refer to the sire and "out of" when they are referring to the dam. After stating the year in which the sire was born, the rest of the summary will encapsulate his racing and breeding history.

From that point on, the page will be dedicated to the history of dams in successive generations. The first dam is its mother, Debs Angel, the second its grandmother, Good Groomer, and so on. The most significant fact to note is how many dams are listed on the page. It is considered a good sign if there is not enough room to list more than three. That means that the first three generations of dams and their offspring had so many winning races that it took up the whole page. You are looking for a colt that is both "by" and "out of" winning blood.

Prospective buyers are searching for a pedigree with black type. Any horse that won a stakes race will be listed in black or bold type and in all capital letters. The ones in black type with both capital and lower-case letters were placed (second or third) in a stakes race. Black type applies to horses that have won stakes (graded and non-graded) that offer purses up to a certain amount set out by the International Cataloging Standards Committee (other restrictions can apply). The point is, the more black type you see, the clearer it is that the runners in this family not only won but also competed and won among the best.

If you are considering buying a horse that, like the horse in this example, has not yet run, check how its brothers and sisters have done. This information is listed under the first dam, provided she's old enough to have produced previous offspring. In this case, Debs Angel, the dam of our Hip Number 5, has, according to the catalog page, produced six winners from seven runners, three of which are listed. As we will see a bit later, a catalog page for a broodmare also lists her produce record, usually in greater detail. The first dam's produce record can add a little insight to the equation if you are getting ready to put your money on the line.

Let's look at another colt from this sale that sold closer to the bottom (see next page). He's two months younger and doesn't bring the same kind of pedigree to the sales ring.

His sire, Bianconi, offers an outstanding racing record but is an unproven

Hip No.
62   Property of Georgiana Farm   **Barn 10G-H**

Dark Bay or Brown Colt

Dark Bay/Br. Colt
April 25, 2001

- Bianconi
  - Danzig
    - Northern Dancer
    - Pas de Nom
  - Fall Aspen
    - Pretense
    - Change Water
- T. T. Tilloo
  (1990)
  - Track Barron
    - Buckfinder
    - Golden Spike
  - Tilloo Bound
    - Our Native
    - Go South

By **BIANCONI (1995)**, black type winner in England, Racal Diadem S. [G2], etc.; hwt. at 5-7 furlongs in Ireland, 2nd Phoenix Sprint S. [G3]. Brother to Hamas [G1], half-brother to 7 black type winners, including Timber Country [G1] ($1,560,400, champion), Fort Wood [G1], Northern Aspen. His first foals are yearlings of 2002.

1st dam
T. T. TILLOO, by Track Barron. Unraced. Dam of 5 foals of racing age, 4 to race, 3 winners--
    Pic a Little (c. by Piccolino). 3 wins at 2 and 3, $93,162, 2nd ‖ Montclair S. (GG, $7,000).
    Cassi's Pic (g. by Piccolino). 3 wins at 3, $34,458.
    T. T.'s Pic (f. by Piccolino). Winner at 3, $8,603.

2nd dam
TILLOO BOUND, by Our Native. 4 wins at 4 and 5, $49,833. Sister to **SILVINO**. Dam of--
    Tilloola. 9 wins, 3 to 6, $154,919.
    Reunited. Placed at 2 and 3.

3rd dam
GO SOUTH, by Jean-Pierre. Placed at 3. Dam of 7 winners, including--
    SILVINO. Winner at 2 in England, 2nd Tattersalls Middle Park [G1], ‖ 3rd Royal Lodge S. [G2]; 5 wins, $107,202 in N.A., Neshaminy H. (PHA, ‖ $23,970), Grantville S. (PEN, $12,690), Somers Point S. (ATL, ‖ $12,000)-ncr, etc.; winner at 6 in South Africa. Sire.
    Groucho Gaucho. 17 wins, 2 to 7, $377,175. Set ncr at Belmont, 1 1/8 miles ‖ in 1:46.42.
    Southern Freeze. Winner at 3, $3,192. To South Africa. Dam of **Polar** ‖ **View** (in South Africa, 3rd Vaal Platinum 1,400).
    Cuz she's Noactor. Dam of **Bigcuz** (2 wins at 2, placed at 3, 2001, $71,465, 2nd Gasparilla S. [L], TAM, $12,000, etc.).

4th dam
YOU ALL, by Nashua. 4 wins at 2 and 3, $47,222, Ashland S., 2nd Jasmine S. Sister to **SHOO DEAR** (dam of **LEPRECHAUNS WISH**, 9 wins, $356,352; **Shoo City Shoo**; g'dam of **WILD WARNING**, $210,061; **BERU**, $188,146; **Wild Wish, Breezy Beru**). Dam of 4 winners, including **HUSH DEAR** (11 wins, $428,458, Long Island H.-**G2** twice, dam of **NOACTOR, Prime Rate Powers**, $121,392; **Touch Judge** [G3]; granddam of **Mountain Bird** [G2], at 3, 2001, $147,838), **PLAINS AND SIMPLE** (dam of **Yankee Axe**), **Salud y Pesetas**. Granddam of **Will to Reign** (24 wins, $440,096).

Eligible for KTDF registration.   12-01

sire. That is, as his first offspring won't race for at least another year, we don't know whether he has the capacity to "throw off" his ability to his heirs. This colt's dam, T. T. Tilloo, was not raced. In spite of that, she foaled several winners, including one who placed in a stakes, but they weren't competing in top races and didn't win much money. Therefore, as you can see, those who prepared the catalog had to continue their search through four generations to find enough information to fill the page. All of these factors play into how much a buyer will be willing to gamble on an untested horse. And for colts, either they win big money at racing or they have a much smaller chance at a breeding future. For this reason, some investors prefer to gamble on a filly with a good pedigree. Even if she is only a mediocre runner, there is a chance that if well mated she can produce winners and bring in revenue that way. And of course, if she can run like the wind, she will be a gold mine.

Let's now turn our attention to the sales page of a broodmare (see next page). Joying brought the single highest price at the Kentucky winter sale, and for good reason.

Just look at that pedigree! Storm Cat has been one of the best sires in racing history. And now look at the produce records of her dam, Jump With Joy, and grandam, Leaping Lucy. This is a very solid record. Her catalog page has been completely filled with winners, and more importantly with plenty of black type, looking no further than two generations.

One question comes to mind. Why would anyone sell such a mare? There are, of course, many possible answers. Maybe the owner needs cash, and this is how he or she is going to get it. Perhaps the sale is just a reduction in inventory. The list goes on, but without speculating further let's look at the rest of the page.

Joying didn't race as a two-year-old and had only moderate success in her third year, although she did place in two minor stakes. She was retired to serve as a broodmare in her fourth year. In the next three years, she produced a foal each year. The first foal, Joy Ridge, and second foal, Finn McCool, achieved modest success, but the third foal, Stunning Success, did not race. Without further investigation, we don't know why.

In 1999 she failed to get pregnant, and in 2001 the foal died. "Aha!" A

Barn 9A-C

Consigned by
David and Ginger Mullins (Doninga), Agent

Hip No.
113

Joying

By STORM CAT (1983), [G1] $570,610. Sire of 12 crops, 91 black type winners, $49,584,269, including Cat Thief [G1] ($3,951,012), Tabasco Cat [G1] ($2,347,671), Giant's Causeway [G1]. Sire of dams of black type winners Phalaenopsis, Black Tuxedo, Max's Pal, Berg Ticket, Baptize, Mujahid, Penny's Gold, Field Cat, Windrush, etc.

1st dam
JUMP WITH JOY, by Linkage. 6 wins, 3 to 5, $110,004, Celosia S. [R] (PHA, $12,720), 2nd Bourbonette S. (TP, $8,630), 3rd Queen S. (TP, $3,845). Sister to **ROYAL LINKAGE**. Dam of 8 foals of racing age, 7 to race, all winners, including--
- WASHINGTON COLOR (c. by Black Tie Affair-IRE). 7 wins, 2 to 5, placed at 8, 2002 in Japan, Garnet S., Yukan Fuji Sho Crystal Cup, Tokyo Chunichi Sports Hai Negishi S. twice, 2nd Takamatsunomiya Kinen, Unicorn S., Tokyo Hai twice, 3rd Sprinters S.
- Little Hans (c. by Hansel). 3 wins in 5 starts at 3 and 4, 2001, $103,600, 2nd Westchester H. [G3].
- Joying (f. by Storm Cat). Black type placed winner, see below.
- Summer Squeal (c. by Summer Squall). 12 wins, 3 to 8, 2001, $361,048.
- Asakusa Kinipary (c. by Kingmambo). Winner at 3, 2002 in Japan.

2nd dam
LEAPING LUCY, by Restless Native. Placed. Half-sister to **LUCY'S AXE** ($208,413). Dam of 7 winners, including--
- JUMP WITH JOY (f. by Linkage). Black type winner, see above.
- ROYAL LINKAGE (f. by Linkage). 2 wins in 4 starts at 2, $49,500, Colleen S. [L] (MTH, $30,000). Dam of 3 winners, including--
  - Royal Fact (f. by Known Fact). 3 wins at 3, 2001, $176,263, 2nd La Lorgnette S. [L] (WO, $22,440), 3rd Selene S. [G1].
- Native Turn To (c. by Transworld). 14 wins, 2 to 7 in Panama, 3rd Premio Republica de Chile [G3].
- Native Lingo (f. by Verbatim). Placed at 2 and 3, 2nd Desert Vixen H. Dam of **Dans Lingo** (f. by Do It Again Dan) $127,477.

Race Record: At 2, unraced; at 3, one win, once 2nd (Vallejo S. [L], GG, $10,000), twice 3rd (Champagne Shower H., GG, $4,500). Earned $27,325.
Produce Record: 1999 not pregnant.
1996 Joy Ridge, f. by Cox's Ridge. 2 wins at 2, $22,661.
1997 **Finn McCool**, c. by Meadowlake. Winner at 3 and 4, 2001, $56,960, 2nd W. Meredith Bailes Memorial S.-R (CNL, $8,000).
1998 Stunning Success, c. by Candy Stripes. Unraced.
2000 Deputy Dog, c. by French Deputy; 2001 foal died.
Last mated March 24, 2001 and **BELIEVED TO BE PREGNANT** to--
OLD TRIESTE (1995) (A.P. Indy--Lovlier Linda), black type winner of 6 races, $847,944, Swaps S. [G2], Californian S. [G2], Del Mar Breeders' Cup H. [G2], Affirmed H. [G3], 2nd Norfolk S. [G2], 3rd Del Mar Breeders' Cup [G2], etc. His first foals are yearlings of 2002.   12-01

non-producing broodmare is only good for consuming food, generating maintenance expense, and requiring new stud fees. This may be the reason the current owner has decided to let someone else gamble on her ability to reproduce. Playing the devil's advocate, however, she did produce four foals. And if she carried a foal by the right sire to term, what then? The final paragraph in bold type now tempts us further that she is believed to be pregnant to Old Trieste, a grade II stakes winner with potential.

So assuming you had the investment wherewithal, what would you do in this case? The buyer at this sale felt she was worth $190,000. Again, it all depends on who you are as an investor and what you are trying to accomplish. This mare is only eleven years old. If the buyer can get her to produce foals, she is good for another eight to ten years of breeding. And with that pedigree? Well, we'll see.

Each of these factors affects the selling price. Even if you are purchasing a horse privately, or by claiming it at a racetrack, you will want to study the pedigree of that individual and probably of its dam to get a good idea of whether it is worth the price.

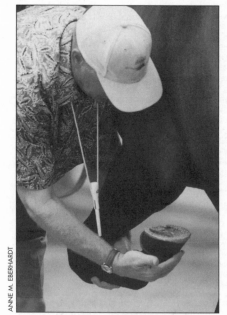

The catalog is a wonderful and invaluable tool to help you decide. Just remember that those who produce the catalog are putting the horse's best hoof forward and will extol every attribute possible. It is the interpretation of the data, as well as what cannot be seen on those pages, that separates the astute from the obtuse. If this is your first venture, obtain a professional's help.

Examining the Inventory

Armed with your well-marked catalog and a list of prospects, you are now ready to start look-

A close-up look at a sale prospect.

ing. The catalog will state the date the horses will be available for viewing. This is usually at least two days before the sale begins. It will save time if you can organize your list so you can progress from successive barns. If there is a crowd at a particular barn, you can always come back. There may be instances in which you will want to return to reconsider a prospect. Please don't overuse this privilege, however, as the horses are in and out of the barn all day and can become exhausted.

If questions have come to mind about things that the catalog page doesn't cover, make a list. Are you concerned about the horse's health, its production record, its previous foals, or whatever? Make a note of those things. Then, when you visit the horse and talk to the consignor you can fill in those blanks, which will help you make a better decision.

Once the sale begins, and the bidding gets underway, it is just impossible to anticipate what will happen. One horse you may have your eye on could suddenly receive offers that go way beyond your budget. If you've not been at an auction, you should be forewarned that your emotions can take control and you may find yourself tempted to violate your financial limits. Don't let this happen. There are many other options, and you must remember that you are looking for a bargain. There is little value in paying an expensive premium from which you may not be able to recoup.

Placing Your Bid

The only thing you must have to buy a horse at a public auction is the money. You need not be a licensed horseman, as is the case of claiming a horse at a track. After buying the horse, you still will not need to worry about licensing until you are ready to enter your horse into a race. Although you may come prepared with certified checks, it is easier to establish a credit line with the auction house before you bid. Instructions on how to do this are included in the catalog.

Even if you aren't ready to buy, if you get a chance to attend an auction by all means do so. Investing a couple of days at a major sale will prove invaluable to your education as a new owner. In addition to the process described above, think of the people you can meet!

The three places you are most likely to find experienced horsemen are at the track, the horse farm, and at an auction. Introduce yourself and explain that you are new and are trying to get a handle on the business. Ask others about their experiences, what they look for, and what criteria they use to make their decisions. In just a short while, you will pick up on how others think and how their perspective affects their decision. You can acquire a decent education in just a few days.

Whenever you purchase a Thoroughbred, you must know exactly when the horse becomes your property. There have been cases in which a new owner bought a horse, paid for it, and signed the contract. Then before the new owner actually received the horse, it got hurt. Now, who owns the faulty property? Specific rules and laws govern this issue, so be sure you understand them. You may even want to purchase special insurance to cover such possibilities. At an auction, the rule is always the same: when the auctioneer's gavel falls, announcing that an entry is sold, the deal is complete and the horse has a new owner. Should the horse have a heart attack or break its leg going out the door, it's the new owner's problem. As a general rule, all horses are sold on an as-is basis.

Even if you later discover that the horse is sick or has an internal malady, there may be little you can do about it. If you are concerned about this kind of problem, you may ask for a complete veterinary examination of the horse before the auction begins. This must be done with the current owner's permission and, of course, you must pay for this costly procedure. It is not normally called for, but when purchasing an especially valuable animal whose family may have had genetic problems, you may want to consider it.

The other side of attending an auction occurs when you have stock to sell. Imagine the anxiety, anticipation, and thrill for those in this position. Just like at the races when it's your horse running for the finish line, your adrenaline will soar as you watch your horse being bid upon. A lot of preparation and planning have gone into the staging for this event in an effort to maximize profit.

Each owner will have given thought as to which sale he or she wants to enter, will have trained the horse in practice sessions to stand and behave before the crowd, and will have groomed the animal "to the nines." Any unsightly hair is trimmed, the mane and tail are shaped and brushed, the hooves are polished, and the horse is treated as carefully as possible to encourage the best mood possible. An auction is a beauty pageant; this is prepping for the judges.

Some animals will not sell at the top prices hoped for. It can be downright disappointing to have your horse in the sales ring and see the auctioneer struggle even to get the bidding started. Every seller must therefore be prepared, if need be, to relinquish the horse at less than the hoped-for estimate. But what if the owner can't afford to sell at a loss?

To protect against such a catastrophe, the current owner may either take part in the bidding (which is allowed) or set a reserve dollar amount under which the horse will not be sold. In the former case, the current owner continues to raise the bid, hoping to push it beyond the minimum. If the owner offers the winning bid, he or she simply signs a sheet stating ownership. In the latter case, if the dollar amount is not reached, the horse will not sell. On the results sheet, after the sale, the letters RNA, or "reserve not attained" will appear. In either case, the owner still pays the auction house a commission for offering the horse for sale. The owner also has incurred all the incidental costs of transporting and caring for the horse during the sale. Each owner must bear this risk in mind before making a consignment to a sale.

There are times, it's sad to say, when an owner can no longer afford a certain animal and will let it go at any price. Some buyers attend an auction looking for just such a situation. They may acquire a valuable Thoroughbred for just a few hundred or a few thousand dollars. Most of these horses, however, may never see a racetrack again. They may be used as show horses, riding horses, or sometimes for the dismal destination of the slaughterhouse. No one wants or likes this, but there is a point at which it makes no sense to continue to put more money into a particular animal. So it will be sold for its best and highest use. And sometimes, that's not very lofty.

The most important outcome after buying a horse is that you go away feeling good about your purchase. You certainly want the best horses you can afford, but you always want to feel that you walked away with a bargain. You have a very good chance of doing that if you take the steps outlined above. More than one person has bid higher than he intended and later felt buyer's remorse. Not because the horse he bought wasn't good, it's just that he overpaid.

The sale of horses at auction is one of the key components in this business. Don't miss a chance to be present even if you're not yet ready to participate. If you aren't sure if you are ready to buy, leave your money at home. You don't want to come home wearing a sheepish grin and have to say, "Guess what, honey…"

Conclusion

More people own racehorses in partnership than ever before. The number of new owners increases every year as novices discover how they can enjoy the thrill of racing their own horses without the need to spend a fortune. Owning what amounts to a sports franchise for such a minimal investment is a rare opportunity.

Long-term success, however, comes by giving the process sufficient time. The now super-successful trainer Bob Baffert tells in his book *Dirt Road to the Derby* about how owner Bob Lewis and another super-successful trainer, D. Wayne Lukas, got started in business together. "Wayne had talked to Bob about giving him a three-year plan. That's when I learned that you can't do anything in one year; it takes three years to really get the ball rolling. If you get lucky after three years and buy the right kind of horses, they should start paying for themselves."

Even when investing at the lower levels, it is essential to consider the whole picture. One quality that allows horsemen to stay in this game year after year is the ability to take a hard knock. Can you do that? The wins are super, but they are not as frequent as the losses.

You must be resilient. If you treat your racing interest as a business, you won't lose too much too fast. Then when your winners come through, your investment becomes worthwhile. Owning a Thoroughbred racehorse is one of the most pleasurable businesses in the world. If you possess the temperament to stick with it, you will surely one day stand with your horse in the winner's circle. Who knows? One of your horses could even be the winner of a hundred-thousand-dollar stakes race. Then there's the Kentucky Derby. So keep dreaming. Opportunity waits for those who do.

Appendix A

How Racing Works

North American Racetracks

There are eighty-nine Thoroughbred racetracks, fifty-one harness tracks, and more than five hundred simulcast outlets across North America. In 2002 there were 61,933 races in North America.

States Holding the Largest Number of Contests

1. California
2. West Virginia
3. Pennsylvania
4. Florida
5. New York
6. Ohio
7. Illinois
8. Louisiana
9. Kentucky
10. Arizona
11. Maryland
12. Texas
13. Massachusetts
14. New Jersey
15. New Mexico

To look tracks up on the Internet, log onto *Daily Racing Form* at www.drf.com. If you aren't familiar with the names and locations of the individual tracks, you can get a listing by state at the National Thoroughbred Racing Association's site, www.ntraracing.com.

To look up racing dates at a track near you or if you'd like to visit a track while on vacation or a business trip, try www.equibase.com. You can print out a schedule of all the races at all the tracks across the country.

How the Racing Industry Works

Each racing meet is sponsored and supported by three organizations that work together closely: the local racing association, The Jockey Club, and the state racing commission. Each plays a role and acts as a balance to the other two.

Local Racing Associations

Racetracks are independently owned and are referred to as local racing associations. The owner may be an individual or family, a for-profit or not-for-profit corporation, or a public agency. Although they have similar objectives, each may vary in how it carries out its business while attempting to provide the best racing competition possible.

There is much more involved in operating a racetrack than just selling tickets and concessions. First, there is the business of attracting the best horses and horsemen, which means providing comfortable facilities to house and care for the horses, designing well-matched races in which the horsemen can make a profit, managing all the betting machines and the books, and adhering to gambling regulations.

Then there is the entertainment side of the business. Fans will only return to the track if they have fun. Watching the horses and gambling provide most of that, but a great many other forms of entertainment are provided by each track. This plethora of activities can range from seminars on handicapping to infield entertainment especially attractive to families with children to outdoor concerts. The local racing association must also work with The Jockey Club, which supervises all Thoroughbred racing in the country, and the state racing commission that issues its license. Each of these three organizations provides a steward for the racing meet, and these stewards have the final authority in making all judgments about the rules and behavior of those who participate in racing.

In addition to stewards, the following officials also will be found at the track:

Racing secretary: This official recruits horses and trainers and puts together the races that are published in the condition book in an attempt to provide competitive races for all the horses registered at the track.

Paymaster of purses: This person handles all monies and accounting that pertain to the racing of horses. That includes all receipts coming in and disbursement going out: fees for nominations, entrance fees, licensing fees and the like, as well as purses, awards, jockey's pay, etc.

Paddock judge: Supervises all aspects of preparing the horses and their riders prior to each race, including the saddling and equipment used on each horse.

Horse identifier: Assists the paddock judge by checking each horse that enters the paddock before a race to ensure that its lip tattoo, markings, and coloring match its registration with The Jockey Club.

Clerk of scales: Oversees the jockey's room, especially the total weight the jockeys carry both before and after a race. This procedure was adopted to guarantee that a dishonest jockey had not secretly carried extra weight when checking in and then disposed of it before the starting gate opened so that his horse ran with a lighter weight.

Official starter: This person watches the horses load into the starting gate. When the horses appear to have settled so none will be at a distinct disadvantage, he or she presses a button that allows the spring-loaded gates to fly open.

Patrol and placing judges: Standing high on top of platforms placed around the perimeter of the track, you will see the patrol judges watching all the activity through binoculars. They are in contact with the stewards if they see anything amiss or if the stewards request their input. The placing judges sit at the wire and make a judgment about the order of the finishers. If it is too close to be obvious, they will post a "photo finish" on the tote board. The stewards will then review the videotapes and photos before making the final decision.

The Jockey Club

Located in Lexington, Kentucky, The Jockey Club was founded in 1894 and has grown into a very large and diverse organization. Its primary responsibility is to serve as the breed registry and to maintain the *American Stud Book*. The organization also works with jockey clubs and registries in other countries.

The Jockey Club publishes a *Fact Book* each year in which statistical summaries are reported. It also offers statistics pertaining to many areas of racing. In addition the staff writes the rules and regulations that most state racing commissions use to govern horsemen. This is an extensive undertaking. And then each year, tens of thousands of foals are born, the ownership of many horses changes, new owners get licensed, and the statistics for all the trainers and jockeys in these countries must be updated. It is a colossal but necessary undertaking, providing information that will help determine the future of this sport.

The State Racing Commission

The governor of each state appoints a racing commission that grants licenses to local racing authorities and horsemen: owners, trainers, jockeys, grooms, veterinarians, and anyone else requiring a license. Commissioners also assign racing dates to each local racing authority. Dates are very important and dynamically affect each locale. Not only must the commission balance the various types of racing meets, such as Thoroughbred, harness, and Quarter Horse, it must consider what takes place in other jurisdictions to ensure that trainers can race year-round.

In large metropolitan areas like New York or Los Angeles, the assigned dates for the major tracks may extend for a long period, in fact operating for the majority of the year. The reason is that the demographic base is large enough to support that effort. In smaller communities the racing meet may be limited to just a few weeks a year. A balance must be struck in providing racing for the fans while at the same time understanding the needs of owners and trainers who must be able to move their stock in an efficient manner.

Licensing

The most important rule for those reading this book is to obtain and carry an active owner's license. Virtually everyone at the racetrack that comes even close to the horses must be licensed. This includes the hotwalkers, grooms, exercise riders, jockeys, trainers, agents, veterinarians, every track official, and, of course, you.

Most states require that anyone owning 5 percent or more of a Thoroughbred must be licensed. That means that every member of your partnership will have to get one. To acquire a license, you will have to obtain an application from the track at which your horse resides, fill out a form, have your picture taken, and be fingerprinted. A standard background check is done to ensure you do not have a criminal record or have not committed an offense within the horse racing industry. If you don't live in that state, all this can be done in your absence to fulfill the legal requirements, but you will not be issued a physical license until you show up with a picture ID to be photographed. Once all that is done, you will be issued a laminated license similar to your driver's license.

Licensing and What It Provides

It's a good feeling to carry an owner's license. The first privilege you will enjoy is permission to visit the stables without having to sign in as a guest. Even if you carry a license, please never enter a barn area without the trainer's permission. You are free to walk around, go where you'd like, talk to the trainers and jockeys, and so on. Make yourself at home. But it is rude to enter a shed row if those people don't know you. If it's your first appointment with a trainer or staff person in a certain stall area, go right up to the first person you see in the area, introduce yourself, and ask for the person you seek. Offering this courtesy and respect will go a long way in your being welcomed everywhere.

At most tracks in the United States, your horseman's license will allow you free entrance to the clubhouse. If you want a reserved seat, of course, you will still have to pay the going rate.

The first time you visit a track, go to the racing secretary's office and introduce yourself. At some tracks, the officials will require a sticker, affixed to the front of your license, to let the gate guards know you have registered. You may not be allowed onto the backside without it.

While at the racing office, you can pick up publications and information not commonly made available to the public. This is where you would pick up a current condition book as well as a listing of jockeys and trainers. The public relations office normally publishes a media guide each year. This guide is prepared specifically for the press and carries plenty of information about the track's history, the stakes races during that meet, and the outstanding achievements of the riders and trainers who frequent that track. Identify yourself as an owner and see if you can get a copy.

The Condition Book

This booklet is prepared every ten days or so by the racing secretary to alert trainers and owners of upcoming races for which their horses may qualify. It also states the conditions for each race and the rules and procedures that the trainers and their staff must follow. If this is the first condition book you've seen, you may want to skim through it to get the general idea, and then plan to spend more time with it later. As the book is written for professional trainers — held accountable to those regulations — many of the terms and references will be unfamiliar.

The important thing to remember when you look at a condition book is that the owners and trainers have to decide about entering their horse in a race several days ahead of time and before they know which horses they will compete against.

The condition book helps the trainer find not only races in which he might enter his horse, but also those that may present an advantage, or better-than-average reward, for his charge.

Types of Races

As explained in chapter 3, the purpose of a **claiming** race is to provide an opportunity for an owner to run his horse in races where the claiming price is high enough to give him fair market value for his horse if it's claimed but low enough to provide his horse with like competition so that it has a chance of winning. When a horse moves up to compete against horses for a higher claiming price, it is said to move up in class. A claimed horse is automatically moved up and must run for a 25 percent higher price if run within thirty days of its acquisition or until that particular meet ends.

Allowance races represent the next step up. Horses with outstanding ability — but not yet up to the best handicapping standards — may compete in these races. Most horses will be "allowed" (from the required normal) a stated reduction in the weight they must carry around the track. Horses that meet more of the stated conditions will not be allowed much, if any, weight concession. Allowance races provide owners and trainers an excellent way to test an untried horse without risking its loss in a claiming race. These races are also a good playing field for quality horses not capable of competing at the higher ranks.

Handicap races are designed for the best horses at the track. As we will see, they reflect the flip side of the allowance race. To level the field, they add weight to horses that have proven themselves better. These races generally offer the largest purses and are announced far in advance so owners or trainers can submit entries in time. Signing up for handicapped races is called "nominating." Some handicaps, called "overnights," close a specific number of hours (ex: 48) before racing.

In the allowance race, the amount of weight allowed is stated in the written conditions of the race before the horses are entered. There are no surprises for the owner or trainer. In a handicap race, however, the racing secretary studies the record of each horse nominated and compares it with the others. After their relative abilities are judged, a weight is assigned and posted just days ahead of time. Now the owners and trainers will discuss whether to enter their horse in that race under those conditions. If they agree to do so, they will take the next step and formally enter it.

All **stakes** races are handicap races, but not all handicap races are stakes races. A stakes race is any race in which owners put up a portion of the purse money in the form of nominating, entrance, and starting fees. In addition to these accumulated fees, or stakes, some races will post a certain amount of added money. These funds come from the local racing association and can range from a few thousand to hundreds of thousands of dollars.

Winning a stakes races is every owner's goal. It represents the top echelon of the sport and means that you have discovered an outstanding individual. If that horse can win several stakes races, especially the more famous ones, it can contend for a championship and buoy you to lofty heights. Not only are the purses at that level worth a lot of money, your horse's breeding value can skyrocket. This is the discovery of that rare diamond.

American Graded Stakes

It is entirely likely that if you stay in this game long enough, you will one day find yourself with one or more horses able to compete at the higher levels. The hundreds of stakes contested each year are placed in three categories, with grade I the highest. The American Graded Stakes Committee, appointed by the Thoroughbred Owners and Breeders Association, assigns grades to stakes races each year. The committee uses a number of criteria for screening races, including a purse requirement of not less than $75,000 for a grade III race; $100,000 for a grade II race; and $125,000 for a grade I race. They further divide these graded races into divisions for horses of various ages, distances, and so forth. Stakes that are not graded are referred to as listed stakes.

The Triple Crown

The Triple Crown consists of the Kentucky Derby, the Preakness Stakes, and the Belmont Stakes. These races, limited to three-year-olds, are run every year, beginning with the Kentucky Derby on the first Saturday in May and ending with the Belmont in early June. All are distance races going a mile and quarter, a mile and three-sixteenths, and a mile and a half, respectively. To win the Triple Crown, one horse must win all three races, a feat that has only been accomplished eleven times in history and not since 1978. Horses that accomplished this feat became well known: Affirmed (1978), Seattle Slew (1977), Secretariat (1973), Citation (1948), and so on.

Both the prestige and the large purses often draw more contenders than the field can accommodate. To meet the requirements to run in the Kentucky Derby, a horse must qualify with sufficient wins resulting in both cumulative purse money and points earned in stakes races. These elements attest to its ability and earn it the right to compete with the best in the field. Additionally, each horse must have been nominated to the Triple Crown races with a six hundred-dollar fee by January of that year. Late nominees pay a heftier late fee.

The Breeders' Cup

The Breeders' Cup is Thoroughbred racing's only year-round national stakes program in which designated races receive extra funding from the Breeders' Cup organization. The Breeders' Cup also is known more popularly as a late-season championship day of eight races. Conceived by breeder John R. Gaines, the Breeders' Cup held its first championship day in 1984.

To participate in Breeders' Cup races, each foal must be nominated to the program by October 15 of its first year with a nomination fee of five hundred dollars. In addition, these foals must be the offspring of nominated stallions. Horses that were not nominated as foals or whose sires were not nominated must pay substantial supplements to run in the year-end championship events. In 2002 more than 13,800 foals were nominated to the Breeders' Cup, bringing in revenue of more than $6.9 million.

Throughout the year horses all across the country compete in the Breeders' Cup series of stakes races. The generous purses are not the only incentive. The nominator of each foal and stallion, even if he or she no longer owns the animal, receives an additional 5 percent nominator award each time that foal runs first, second, or third in any Breeders' Cup-sponsored event. That's quite a motivation.

The Breeders' Cup World Thoroughbred Championship takes place in the fall at a different host track and showcases the best horses from America and even some from Europe for that year. The eight races offer total purses of thirteen million dollars, culminating in the four-million-dollar Breeders' Cup Classic.

The Eclipse Awards

The Eclipse Awards are determined each year by votes from members of the National Thoroughbred Racing Association, the National Turf Writers Association, and *Daily Racing Form*. The awards recognize the outstanding people and horses for a particular year. The awards are named after the eighteenth-century horse, Eclipse, who began racing at age five, was undefeated in eighteen starts, and went on to become one of the foundation sires of the American Thoroughbred.

Awards are given for Horse of the Year; champion two-year-old colt and filly; three-year-old colt and filly; older male and female; male and female turf runner; sprinter, and steeplechaser. Awards are also given to those people who stand out among their peers as outstanding owner, breeder, jockey, apprentice jockey, trainer, and member of the media. These recipients stand out as the finest in each class, elected by those who know the sport best.

Appendix B

Examples of Bills

The following sample is an actual billing from a farm in Maryland where the author had four horses in partnership. The farm owner/managing partner was overseeing the breeding stock partnership as well as the horses that were racing and in training.

Jovial Joy was a broodmare; 01 Jovial Joy was a foal born in 2001 and not yet named; Churchontime was a filly in training; and Sunshine in Paris was a filly racing at local tracks.

Note the following:

• The variety of charges and how they differ for each horse.

• The higher cost when a horse is racing, as was the case with Sunshine in Paris.

• The difference in the day rate at each facility. Churchontime was at a training facility in Middleburg at a rate of $40 per day.

• Maybe most importantly, for a fraction of the total cost the author was able to own a percentage in four horses that diversified the risk of involvement.

Monthly Statement
Period Ending: 12/31/2001
Page 1
Client Summary

	Charges	Credits	Balance
PREVIOUS BALANCE:			$420.30
Payments received 12/17/2001		$420.30	
Check No: 5305			
BEGINNING BALANCE:			
Current Month Horses Charges			
Jovial Joy	$259.02		
01 Jovial Joy	$234.90		
Churchontime	$75.30		
Sunshine in Paris	$605.90		
Total Horse Charges:	$1,175.12		
ENDING BALANCE:			$1,175.12

Monthly Statement
Period Ending: 12/31/2001
Page 2
Jovial Joy

Date	Description	Total Charge	Owner Percent	Owner Portion
12/01/01	Thru 12/31/01 Board @ $20.00	$620.00	10.00%	$62.00
12/01/01	Mortality Insurance Premium	$1,313.00	10.00%	$131.30
	$25,000—Coverage 9/30/01 through 9/30/02			
12/01/01	Liability Insurance Premium	$492.00	10.00%	$49.20
12/31/01	Management Fee	$100.00	10.00%	$10.00
12/31/01	Cimetidine Treatment			
	49 days—Nov 13 thru Dec 31	$65.20	10.00%	$6.52
		$2,590.20		$259.02

Monthly Statement
Period Ending: 12/31/2001
Page 3
Jovial Joy

Date	Description	Total Charge	Owner Percent	Owner Portion
12/01/01	Thru 12/31/01 Board @ $20.00	$620.00	10.00%	$62.00
12/01/01	Thru 12/31/01 Board @ $14.00	$434.00	10.00%	$43.40
12/01/01	Mortality Insurance Premium	$1,245.00	10.00%	$124.50
	$50,000—Coverage 9/30/01 through 9/30/02			
12/22/01	Equi-stem	$15.00	10.00%	$1.50
12/22/01	Banamine	$10.00	10.00%	$1.00
12/22/01	Vet Call—Fever	$30.00	10.00%	$3.00
12/23/01	Penicillin—2 Doses	$12.00	10.00%	$1.20
12/31/01	MD Million Nomination	$250.00	10.00%	$25.00
12/31/01	Sulfamethazole-Trimethoprim DS			
	7-day Treatment	$28.00	10.00%	$2.80
12/31/01	Farm Registration Processing	$75.00	10.00%	$7.50
12/31/01	Jockey Club Registration Fee	$200.00	10.00%	$20.00
12/31/01	MD Bred Registration	$50.00	10.00%	$5.00
		$2,349.00		$234.90

Monthly Statement
Period Ending: 12/31/2001
Page 4
Churchontime

Date	Description	Total Charge	Owner Percent	Owner Portion
12/01/01	Vanning—			
	Middleburg to Timonium	$150.00	5.00%	$7.50
12/01/01	Training & Board—			
	Middleburg—1 day	$40.00	5.00%	$2.00
12/01/01	Hind Shoes & Trim—			
	n/c 11/15/01	$52.00	5.00%	$2.60
12/01/01	Mortality Insurance Premium	$451.00	5.00%	$22.55
	$80,000—Coverage 9/30/01 through 12/01/01			
12/01/01	Liability Insurance Premium	$90.00	5.00%	$4.50
	Coverage 9/30/01 through 12/02/01			
12/01/01	Palp & Spec—Sales Expense	$33.00	5.00%	$1.65
12/01/01	Vet Exam 11/13/01	$40.00	5.00%	$2.00
12/01/01	Vet Work—Sonogram	$100.00	5.00%	$5.00
12/01/01	Accounting Fees	$550.00	5.00%	$27.50
		$1,506.00	5.00%	$75.30

Monthly Statement
Period Ending: 12/31/2001
Page 5
Sunshine in Paris

Date	Description	Total Charge	Owner Percent	Owner Portion
12/01/01	Mortality Insurance Premium	$3,380.00	10.00%	$338.00
	$100,000—Coverage 9/30/01 through 9/30/02			
12/01/01	Liability Insurance Premium	$518.00	10.00%	$51.80
12/31/01	Blacksmith—Track	$95.00	10.00%	$9.50
12/31/01	Worm	$15.00	10.00%	$1.50
12/31/01	Training and Board—Bowie	$1,705.00	10.00%	$170.50
12/31/01	Management Fee	$100.00	10.00%	$10.00
12/31/01	Veterinary Work—Track	$246.00	10.00%	$24.60
	Vitamins, Minerals, Bute, Lasix, etc.			
		$6,059.00		$605.90

Monthly Statement
Period Ending: 12/31/2001
Page 6
Charge Type Summary

	Total Charge	*Owner Portion*
Total Board	$1,054.00	$105.40
Total Blacksmith	$52.00	$2.60
Total Insurance	$6,389.00	$616.35
Total Medicine	$108.20	$10.82
Total Miscellaneous	$1,850.00	$153.00
Total Nominations	$250.00	$25.00
Total Registrations	$325.00	$32.50
Total Training & Track Charges	$2,186.00	$211.60
Total Vanning	$150.00	$7.50
Total Veterinary	$140.00	$10.35
Horse Total	$12,504.20	$1,175.12

Appendix C

Sample Written Agreement

(**Note**: The author obtained a generic sample agreement of a Limited Liability Company [LLC] that helps to point out the main areas every agreement should contain. The entire document is too lengthy [and boring] to include in its entirety, but the main sections and points are included here to stimulate the reader's thoughts about the issues to discuss with his advisers and managing partner. Nonetheless, the content of the omitted sections is indicated.)

LIMITED LIABILITY COMPANY

OPERATING AGREEMENT

OF

_____, LLC

THIS LIMITED LIABILITY COMPANY OPERATING AGREEMENT (the "Agreement") is made and entered into as of ____, 2003, by and between _____ ("_____") hereinafter referred to as "Managing Member" or "General Manager," and those persons listed on Exhibit A ("Nonmanaging Members"). _____ and the Nonmanaging Members shall hereinafter be individually referred to as a "Member" and collectively referred to as the "Members."

WITNESSETH

WHEREAS, _____ and the Nonmanaging Members desire to form a limited liability company on the terms and conditions hereinafter provided.

NOW, THEREFORE, in consideration of the mutual premises contained herein and for good and valuable consideration the receipt and adequacy of which is hereby acknowledged, the parties hereto hereby agree as follows:

ARTICLE 1

DEFINITIONS

(**Note**: Text omitted for purposes of this book.)

ARTICLE 2

FORMATION

2.1   Formation. The Members hereby agree to form a limited liability company (the "Company") subject to the terms of this Agreement and in accordance with the provisions of _____law allowing for limited liability companies (the "Act"), and, in connection with the foregoing, the Members will approve the Articles of Organization of the Company, which will be prepared and duly filed in accordance with the laws of _____. The Company will pay the expenses incidental to its formation, including filing costs, accounting and legal fees and direct out-of-pocket expenses.

 2.2   Name. The business and affairs of the Company shall be conducted under the name "_____, LLC," or such other name as the Members may from time to time determine.

2.3   Principal Place of Business. The principal place of business and mailing address of the Company in _____ shall be located at:

_____

_____

or such other additional locations as the Members shall from time to time designate.

2.4   Resident Agent. The registered agent of the Company for service of process in _____shall be _____.

2.5   Objects and Purpose. The Company is organized for the following object and purposes:

_____

_____(the "Business").

2.6   Term. The Company shall continue until December 31, 2052, unless sooner terminated in accordance with the provisions of this Agreement or otherwise dissolved pursuant to the laws of _____.

2.7   Members: Limited Liability.

(a)   The names and addresses of the Members and the amount of the Percentage Interest held by each Member are set forth in Exhibit A attached hereto. Exhibit A attached hereto may be amended from time to time to reflect any change in the identity of Members and/or Percentage Interests.

(b)   No Member shall be liable for the repayment, satisfaction and discharge or any debts, liabilities and obligations of the Company except to the extent required by the Act.

ARTICLE 3
CAPITAL; ADDITIONAL CONTRIBUTIONS; WITHDRAWALS

3.1   Initial Capital Contributions. Simultaneously with the execution of this Agreement, each Member shall contribute as its contribution to the capital of the Company, cash in the amount set forth opposite its name on Exhibit A attached hereto. No Member shall have priority over any other Member, either as to return of its Capital Contribution or as to profits, losses or distributions, except as otherwise specifically provided herein. Moreover, no Member shall be personally liable for the return of the Capital Contribution of any Member, or any portion thereof, it being-expressly understood that any such return shall be made solely from assets of the Company.

3.2   Interest on Contributions. No interest shall be payable on the Capital Contributions made by the Members to the Company.

3.3   Withdrawal of Contributions. Any Capital Contribution may not be withdrawn from the Company without the consent of the Managing Member and a majority-in-interest of the remaining Members.

3.4   Capital Accounts. There shall be maintained for each Member a separate capital account which shall be governed and maintained throughout the term of the Company in accordance with the provisions of Regulation Section 1.704-l(b).

3.5   Loans From Members. A Member may make a loan to the Company on such terms and conditions as the General Manager determines to be fair and reasonable. Any Member who makes a loan to the Company shall (except as may be provided otherwise by the terms and conditions of such loan) have the same rights and obligations with respect to such loan as a person who is not a Member. The amount of a loan, if any, made to the Company, or guaranteed or otherwise arranged, by a Member shall not be considered an increase in such Member's Capital Contribution or otherwise constitute a contribution to the Company nor shall the making of such loan entitle such Member to an increased share of the profits, losses, or distributions to be made pursuant to the provisions of this Agreement. No loan shall have an equity participation feature without the consent of Members holding in the aggregate at least a majority of the Membership Interests.

3.6   Interests of Nonrecourse Creditors. A creditor (including a Member) who makes a nonrecourse loan to the Company shall not have or acquire, at any time as a result of making the loan, any direct or indirect interest in the profits, capital or property of the Company other than as a secured creditor.

ARTICLE 4

PROFITS, LOSSES, AND DISTRIBUTIONS

(**Note**: Any agreement should include paragraphs that spell out how profits and losses will be allocated and how frequently they will be distributed to the members. This is also a good place to include any special provisions, such as how to deal with the tax issues of deductibility, gains, losses, etc.)

ARTICLE 5

MANAGEMENT

5.1   Management of the Company. The Company shall be managed by a General Manager. _____is hereby appointed to serve as the initial General Manager.

5.2   General Manager. The business and affairs of the Company shall be managed under the direction and control of the General Manager, and all powers of the Company shall be exercised by or under the authority of the General Manager. No other person or Member shall have any right or authority to act for or bind the Company except as permitted in this Agreement or as required by law.

5.3   Powers and Duties. Subject to the provisions of this Agreement, the General Manager shall have full, exclusive and complete discretion, power and authority to manage, control, administer and operate the business and affairs of the Company for the purposes herein stated, and to make all decisions affecting such business and affairs, including, without limitation, the power to execute and deliver, for and on behalf of the Company, any and all documents and instruments which may be necessary or desirable in order to carry on the business of the Company. Any document or instrument executed and delivered in the name of the Company by the General Manager shall be deemed to have been duly authorized by the Members of the Company.

(**Note**: Additionally, this article might address issues such as restrictions pertaining to the General Manager, his or her removal, limitation of authority of members, compensations, and meetings.)

ARTICLE 6

BOOKS AND RECORDS

6.1   Bank Accounts. All funds of the Company shall be deposited in a bank account or accounts opened in the Company's name. The General Manager shall determine the financial institution or institutions at which the account(s) will be opened and the persons who will have authority with respect to the accounts and funds therein.

6.2   Fiscal Year. The fiscal year of the Company (the "Fiscal Year") shall be the calendar year.

6.3   Books and Records. Complete and accurate books of account shall be kept or caused to be kept by the General Manager of the Company. All of the Company's books of account, together with an executed copy of this Agreement and copies of such other instruments as the General Manager may execute hereunder, including amendments thereto, shall at all times be kept at the business office of the Company, and all such books and records shall be available during normal business hours for inspection by any Member or its duly authorized representative or, at the expense of any Member, for audit by it or its duly authorized representative.

6.4   Tax Matters Partner. The Managing Member shall be the "Tax Matters Partner" as defined in and for all purposes under the Code.

ARTICLE 7

TRANSFER OF INTERESTS

(**Note**: This article should include what occurs if any of the partners want or need to get out of the partnership, whether any interest can be assigned to someone else [with or without the approval of the other members], and whether the other members will be offered first rights of refusal in such a case.)

ARTICLE 8

DISSOLUTION AND LIQUIDATION

(**Note:** This article addresses how dissolution of the partnership will be handled in a manner fair to all parties.)

ARTICLE 9

MISCELLANEOUS

(**Note**: Text omitted for purposes of this book.)

EXHIBIT "A"

(**Note**: In most legal agreements this exhibit will list the owners and the degree of their ownership. In a partnership or LLC agreement for horse owners, Exhibit A should state the name of the managing partner, any capital contribution he or she has made, and the percentage owned. Following that should be a list of the names of all partners [members], the amount of each contribution, and the total percentage interest held.)

Resources

Books, Brochures, Newspapers, and Magazines

Auerbach, Ann Hagedorn. *Wild Ride*. New York: Henry Holt and Company, 1994.

Baffert, Bob with Steve Haskin. *Baffert: Dirt Road to the Derby*. Lexington, KY: Blood-Horse Publications, Inc., 1999. Baffert is a down-to-earth trainer with a great sense of humor.

Blazer, Don. *Make Money With Horses: You Can Do It*. Cave Creek, AZ: Success is Easy, 1998. Excellent at providing guidelines for making a profit within various sectors of racing.

Blood-Horse Publications, P.O. Box 4038, Lexington, KY 40544-4038, Phone: 859-278-2361, Fax: 859-276-6708, www.bloodhorse.com. *The Blood-Horse* magazine is a weekly publication covering the Thoroughbred industry. Its web site covers racing, breeding, handicapping, and ownership. It has a calendar of horse events and much more. It also contains links to a marketplace, publications, and web resources.

Campbell, W. Cothran. *Lightning in a Jar*. Lexington, KY: Eclipse Press, 2000. An excellent inside look at the excitement and business side of owning a racehorse.

Daily Racing Form, 100 Broadway, 7th Floor, New York, NY 10005-1902, Phone: 212-366-7600, www.drf.com. The *Daily Racing Form* is a national racing newspaper that provides up-to-date information on racing as well as statistical information for the beginner and advanced handicapper. DRF online service provides an electronic version of the *Form*.

Del Castillo, Janet. *Backyard Racehorse: The Training Manual. A Comprehensive Off-Track Program for Owners and Training*, 3rd ed. Winter Haven, FL: Prediction Publications & Productions, 1997. Hands-on advice from a hands-on owner/trainer. This book deals primarily with those who have their own facilities and want to train their own horses.

Ivers, Tom. *Complete Guide to Claiming Thoroughbreds: Finding, Fixing and Making Winners*. Menasha, WI: The Russell Meerdink Company, Ltd., 1999. Covers many issues an owner would need to know but is aimed at those who intend to specialize in claiming.

The Jockey Club. *2003 Fact Book*. New York-Lexington: The Jockey Club, 2002.

Internal Revenue Service. *The Official IRS Tax Guide to Auditing Horse Activities*. Menasha, WI: The Russell Meerdink Company, Ltd., 2002.

Kirkpatrick, Arnold. *Investing in Thoroughbreds: Strategies for Success*. Lexington, KY: Eclipse Press, 2001. Written in a winning, friendly voice and covers most of the issues a horseman would need to know.

Taylor, Joseph Lannon. *Joe Taylor's Complete Guide to Breeding and Raising Racehorses*. Neenah, WI: Russell Meerdink, Ltd., 1999. One of the best reference books for owners by a man who has been involved in the Thoroughbred business for years.

Thoroughbred Owners and Breeders Association (TOBA). *The New Thoroughbred Owners Handbook*. Lexington, KY: Eclipse Press, 2003. A comprehensive manual on all aspects of owning Thoroughbreds.

Thoroughbred Owners of California (TOC). *Handbook for Thoroughbred Owners of California*. Arcadia, CA: TOC, 1996. Well-written workbook covering most topics important to Thoroughbred owners.

Thoroughbred Times, 2008 Mercer Road, Lexington, KY 40511, Phone: 859-260-9800, Fax: 859-260-9814, www.thoroughbredtimes.com. *Thoroughbred Times* is a weekly news magazine that covers Thoroughbred breeding and racing. It covers North American stakes results and sales, breeding and pedigree, sire lists, extensive news on leaders in the field, veterinary reports, business issues, and more.

Videotapes

Conformation: How to Buy a Winner. Lexington, KY: The Blood-Horse, 1997.

A Guide to Buying Your Own Racehorse. Wilmington, DE: C&O Commercial Productions, Inc., 1995.

Insider's Guide to Buying Thoroughbreds at Auction. Lexington, KY: The Blood-Horse, 1999.

Owning Thoroughbreds. Lexington, KY: Blood-Horse Publications and the Thoroughbred Owners and Breeders Association, 1998.

Sales Preparation. Lexington, KY: The Blood-Horse, 1999.

Other Resources

Bloodstock Research Information Services, Inc. (BRISnet), P.O. Box 4097, 801 Corporate Drive, 3rd Floor, Lexington, KY 40544, www.brisnet.com. BRISnet is an online service that is a knowledge base of information for the handicapper and horse enthusiast. It provides reports and statistical data on Thoroughbred racing, past performance reports, entries and programs, results and charts, pedigree reports, trainer and jockey reports, and much more. Although there is a fee for many of their reports, the company offers some free services, such as its *Handicapper's Edge* newsletter, *Bloodstock Journal*, and instant race results.

Equibase Company LLC, 821 Corporate Drive, Lexington, KY 40503-2794, www.equibase.com. Equibase gathers and distributes past performance information for Thoroughbred racetracks. Its web site offers any array of handicapping information.

Equine Line 2000, www.equineline.com. This online service launched by The Jockey Club Information Systems allows the subscriber to develop a portfolio of horses, both for

Thoroughbreds and Quarter Horses, which is updated continuously with new information. Individual breeding, racing, and sales reports can be downloaded for a charge.

The Greatest Game, www.thegreatestgame.com. The Thoroughbred Owners and Breeders Association administers and manages The Greatest Game, an educational web site for those interested in buying a Thoroughbred racehorse.

Horsemen's Benevolent and Protective Association (HBPA), The National HBPA, National Horse Center, Building B, Suite 2, 4063 Ironworks Pike, Lexington, KY 40511-8905, Phone: 859-259-0451 or 866-245-1711, www.hbpa.org. HBPA is a non-profit corporation created to improve racing on all levels in the United States and Canada.

The Jockey Club, 821 Corporate Drive, Lexington, KY 40503, Phone: 859-224-2700, Fax: 859-224-2710, www.thejockeyclub.com. The Jockey Club's primary responsibility is maintaining the *American Stud Book*, the registry of all Thoroughbreds foaled in the United States, Canada, and Puerto Rico. Owners and breeders can register their foals online.

The Jockey Club Information Systems (TJCIS), 821 Corporate Drive, Lexington, KY 40503, Phone: 800-333-1778, Fax: 859-224-2810, www.tjcis.com. The TJCIS, a wholly owned subsidiary of The Jockey Club, offers three principal product lines: Catalogue Pages and Specialty Products, Equine Line and Customized Reports, Software Packages and Consulting.

The National Thoroughbred Racing Association (NTRA), 2525 Harrodsburg Road, Lexington, KY 40504, 859-223-5444, Fax: 859-223-394, www.ntra.com. The NTRA and the Breeders' Cup Limited merged in 2001 to provide programs and services to the Thoroughbred industry. The NTRA web site has an abundance of information on every aspect of the racing industry and links to helpful resources.

Thoroughbred Owners and Breeders Association (TOBA), P.O.Box 4367, Lexington, KY 40544-4367, Phone: 859-276-2291, Fax: 859-276-2462, www.toba.org. TOBA is a national organization that supports owners and breeders. Membership benefits include educational seminars; a free subscription to *The Blood-Horse* magazine; the *Stallion Register*; and the TOBA Membership Directory.

Thoroughbred Owners of California (TOC), 285 W. Huntington Drive, Arcadia, CA 91007, Phone: 800-994-9909 (in CA), Phone: 626-574-6620 (out-of-state), www.toconline.com. TOC is an association of California horse owners that works to protect their economic interests and investments. TOC offers free educational seminars.

Index

Index

Acknowledgments

Anyone who writes a book does so with any number of people's help. That is especially true for a first-time author like me. And I would like to say thanks to all those who gave me advice, encouragement, time, or just an arm around the shoulder.

In a chronological order of sorts, I would like to start by thanking my friend Richard Wira for introducing me to the excitement and fun of owning a racehorse in partnership. I had no idea...

Next, my wife, Joan, did so much work to help me, especially at the start. When a person doesn't know what he is doing, which I didn't, he tends to start down many dead ends that consume time and yield little. Thanks for helping with all that.

The trainers, bloodstock agents, track officials, media, farm owners and employees, etc. would be far too numerous to mention. Nonetheless, I thank each of you for your help and input. Although not mentioned by name, I remember and appreciate each of you.

Thanks to Dave Dick, Charles Douglas, and Richard Wagner for the professional help they volunteered. (Note that any topic relating to legal, taxation, or other business issue is put forth as an illustration — not as advice to any individual. Each owner must obtain his or her own professional council.)

My proofreaders who gave of their time and wisdom: Jerry King, Tim Muetzel, Josh Pons, Scott Thomas, and Russ Vuich.

To Al Zuckerman, my agent, thanks for having the courage to take on a novice at this stage of your successful career.

And finally to my editors, Jackie Duke and her staff, thanks for holding my hand and coaching me through the process.

About the Author

Harold Metzel spent much of his life as an administrator and fund-raiser for public charities. In that capacity, he gained much experience in public speaking and in writing for professional publications.

Upon retiring, Metzel aspired to write fiction but became sidetracked when his interest in horse racing led him to discover not much had been written for people with his newly found interest.

Metzel has owned fourteen Thoroughbreds in a variety of

Joan and Harold Metzel

partnerships. He particularly enjoys the breeding aspect of horse ownership. He currently owns partnership interests in a two-year-old in training and in a pregnant broodmare that finished her racing career last fall.

Harold and his wife, Joan, live in the Dallas, Texas, area.